What's with Chicago?

Library of Congress Control Number: 2017957323

ISBN: 9781681061306

All photos, unless otherwise identified, were taken by Richard W. Shubart.

Design by Jill Halpin

Printed in the United States of America
18 19 20 21 22   5 4 3 2 1

DEDICATION

To my family; Chicago is home for all of us,
even those who don't live here.

CONTENTS

PREFACE

Windy City. Second City. Hog Butcher to the World. Well, maybe not that anymore, but Chicago stands tall among world cities, known for, yes, its wind, but also its bluster, its magnificent skyline, its history of architectural excellence, its literature, and its news, art, and industry.

It was a pleasure to write the story of what makes Chicago Chicago. So much more can be said, but in this short book I have tried to give a flavor of my hometown: its food, its streets, its high-rises and supertalls, its spectacular geography that brings us an ocean-sized lake and a river that today jumps and jives, and its unique neighborhoods.

This is not a history. It leaves out a great deal about the development of this complex city. Neither is this a guidebook, as many more places are to be seen in this city than could be listed here. Rather, it's a reflection of a multifaceted city by a lifelong Chicagoan who loves it; no more but also no less.

This book was made possible with the help of two special people. Cliché it is, but without my dear friend Carol, who edited these snippets and made sure they read easily, and my husband, Richard, who took all the photos, this could not have been assembled. Special thanks to both of them.

This book is intended as a dip into the amazing city of Chicago, which, after more than 150 years, has become a cosmopolitan, world-class city while still holding on to its hometown traditions, good and bad. Read on to find out what makes Chicago what it is, and read on to find out about its secrets, its proud heritage, and its foibles. Enjoy!

Ellen Shubart

What's with Chicago?

Ellen Shubart

REEDY PRESS

Hot Diggity

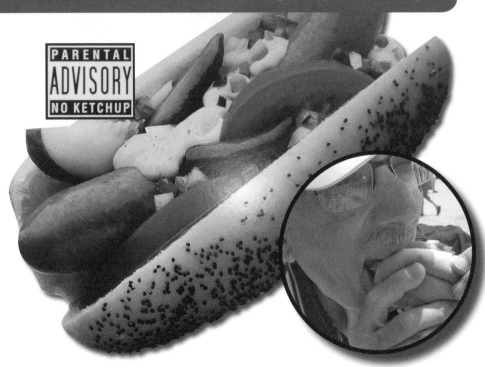

Bite into a Chicago-style hot dog that's been "dragged through a garden" and flavors and textures explode in your mouth: tomato, dill pickle spear, neon-green pickle relish, (hot) sport peppers, diced onion, yellow mustard, and a sprinkle of celery salt. The toppings cover an all-beef, kosher-style sausage nestled in a steamed poppy seed bun. The major caveat: NO KETCHUP!

 FOOD AND DRINK

The sandwich dates to 1893, when the all-beef sausage was introduced at the World's Columbian Exposition in Chicago. Called a "frankfurter," indicating its German origin, it was originally topped only with mustard. It remained a frankfurter until the US went to war against Germany in World War I, when it quickly became a "hot dog."

Finishing touches came during the Great Depression, when vegetables were added to the mustard-topped sausage. Street vendors sold a hot meal for a nickel. Today, hot dog stands, shed-like buildings offering hot dog-and-fries combos, are ubiquitous around the city, easily spotted with their yellow Vienna Beef signs.

Why no ketchup? Some experts theorize that the tomato piquancy would overwhelm the veggies and other condiments.

Kids learn early about the Chicago hot dog's appeal: At the Chicago History Museum, little ones can "become" a hot dog by lying in a fabric-covered "bun" and having pillows representing tomato, pickle, onions, and mustard thrown on top.

Fact BOX

Today, the largest US company producing all-beef, kosher-style hot dogs is also the oldest. Austro-Hungarian immigrants Emil Reichel and Sam Ladany launched Vienna Beef Co. in 1893, introducing their all-beef sausage at the World's Fair in Chicago. The frankfurter appealed to Eastern European Jewish immigrants because it didn't include forbidden pork.

Hot, dipped, and cut

The Italian beef sandwich

Take thinly sliced marinated beef, stack it high on a crusty French roll, top it with roasted sweet peppers or hot gardiniera, add jus, and you have the iconic Chicago Italian beef sandwich.

Created in 1938 at Al's #1 Italian Beef in the city's Little Italy neighborhood, it's still one of Chicago's trademark meals. Al's unique top sirloin is used for superior flavor. Other restaurants may use different cuts of beef.

Servers hold the bun in hand, take a forkful of beef, swish it in the jus, and plop it on the bread. "Wet" sandwiches get jus ladled over the meat; "dipped," the choice of most customers, submerges the bun

FOOD AND DRINK

completely in the jus. The bun, produced by Gonnella Baking Co., another Italian immigrant operation, is created to be dipped without losing its shape.

"Hot" means the addition of gardiniera, a combination of celery and bell peppers marinated in spices, oil, and red pepper flakes to add both a kick and a crunch. "Sweet" brings the roasted peppers. Those in the know add both.

"Cut" sandwiches are finished off with a slice down the middle, making them easier to handle.

Eat up—it's delicious!

Al's founder, Al Ferrari, is said to have created the beef sandwich because he needed to stretch the meat he had to feed a whopping 150 wedding guests. Ferrari started with one shop on Taylor Street in Little Italy. Today, the brand has grown into a chain. At one location, an average day means serving up four hundred Italian beefs, and on a "crazy day," it's six hundred to seven hundred sandwiches.

Buon appetito!

Chicago-style pizza

Deep-dish pizza, now popular far and wide, originated in 1943 at Chicago's Pizzeria Uno. Known as "Chicago style," it is a thick crust filled with mozzarella and Parmesean cheese and such additions as sausage, pepperoni, mushrooms, olives, or spinach, all topped with spicy tomato sauce and baked at a very high temperature for fifty to sixty minutes. The lengthy baking time is possible because the sauce on top keeps the cheese from burning.

Pizza, the thin-crust kind, came to America from Naples, Italy, where in 1889 a chef had created Pizza Margherita, with tomato, mozzarella, and basil representing the colors of the

FOOD AND DRINK

Italian flag. During World War II, G.I.s stationed in Italy became familiar with the ethnic delight and brought home their taste for it. Among the first eateries to capitalize on Americans' love affair with Italian foods were Pizzeria Uno and its sister restaurant, Due, founded on the Near North Side by Ric Riccardo, a local restaurateur, and Ike and Florence Sewell.

Chicago-style pizza is both loved and reviled. In New York, for example, where pizza means a thin triangular slice, comedian Jon Stewart denigrated Chicago's thick-crust version as just a "bowl of tomato sauce." Chicagoans reject that heartily, displaying their loyalty at outlets of restaurant chains throughout the region, including Giordano's, Gino's East, and Lou Malnati's, as well as myriad independent Italian eateries.

Just a meat-and-potatoes town

Chicago's steakhouses

Chicago has always been known as a first-rate expense account town, featuring high-quality fresh beef and the steakhouses that serve it. Beginning in the 1840s, it became known as the last town before the West where businessmen could get a decent meal.

With the advent of the Union Stockyards in the late nineteenth century, freshly slaughtered beef was readily available and became a citywide favorite. By the late twentieth century, various cuts of steak, dry-aged and served up sizzling on a plate with sides of baked potato and creamed spinach, were the city's trademark. For many, the steakhouse is the place to go to splurge or celebrate a special event. To some, it's what gives Chicago its distinctively masculine character.

The city's downtown and Near North Side have possibly the highest concentration of quality beef restaurants anywhere,

FOOD AND DRINK

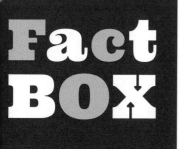

estimated at more than fifty, and most are filled nightly with conventioneers as well as locals.

Not all steakhouses feature the traditional white-tablecloth service anymore, and many have given "meat and potatoes" updated meanings with dishes such as beef cheek poutine or potato funnel cakes. Still, meat and potatoes defines dining Chicago style.

Fact BOX

The Union Stock Yards meatpacking district opened in 1865. The 375-acre site had 2,300 livestock pens, room for 75,000 hogs, 21,000 cattle, and 22,000 sheep. By 1890, Chicago processed 82 percent of the nation's meat. The stockyards closed in 1971. Its gate was designated a Chicago Landmark in 1972 and a National Historic Landmark in 1981.

Ronald McDonald lives in Chicago

McDonald's hamburgers, charities

Despite the name, the hugely successful McDonald's hamburger chain was the brainchild of Ray Kroc. He was the Oak Park, Illinois, native who persuaded the California-based McDonald brothers, operators of a restaurant under their name, to make him sole franchising agent for their proposed chain. In 1955, Kroc opened the first McDonald's, in the Chicago suburb of Des Plaines, and business grew exponentially. Today, McDonald's, with more than thirty-six thousand locations in one hundred countries, is the largest fast-food chain in the United States and the largest restaurant company in the world in terms of both number of customers and revenue.

Hamburger University, home to test kitchens and classrooms, is part of the company's headquarters, which is scheduled to move to

FOOD AND DRINK

downtown Chicago from suburban Oak Brook in 2018.

Ronald McDonald, the chain's primary mascot, was originally seen in television commercials inhabiting McDonaldland, a fantasy world, but he's moved on and today is shown interacting with real children in everyday life.

Ronald also lends his name to the more than 350 Ronald McDonald Houses in forty-two countries, which provide places to stay for parents of children being treated in nearby chronic-care facilities.

The houses are run by Ronald McDonald House Charities, an independent US nonprofit organization dedicated to improving children's health. Its major corporate partner is the McDonald's system of restaurant owners/operators, company employees, and suppliers.

Eating ethnically

From pierogis to jibaritos and more

Chicago has long had a rich ethnic food scene supported by its diverse neighborhoods. You can find Mexican food in Pilsen, Italian food along Taylor Street in Little Italy, East Indian food along the North Side's Devon Avenue, Greek food in Greektown, and Asian food in Chinatown.

Lately, however, even more food diversity is available to enjoy. According to Daniel Gerzina, a writer for the Eater Chicago food website, "Restaurants in the nation's third-largest city have grown to a level of sophistication that rivals any food scene in the country." That means you can find Polish pierogis, Southern-style fried chicken, or German sauerbraten in many areas beyond their traditional ethnic

VOTED CHICAGO'S
★ **BEST** ★
PIEROGI

neighborhoods, and restaurant offerings range from diner style to fine dining.

Lesser-known ethnic specialties can also be found in Chicago, including Danish-influenced cuisine at Elske in the West Loop, churros and Mexican hot chocolate at Xoco in River North, and Costa Rican delicacies at Irazu in Wicker Park. Cafecito, which many say offers the best Cuban food in the Midwest, is lodged in the Harris Family Hostel in downtown Chicago, and Puerto Rican jibaritos are now considered a "modern Chicago classic," according to *Chicago Tribune* food writer Nick Kindelsperger. The sandwiches made with fried plantains in place of bread can be found at many restaurants, including some that don't serve other Puerto Rican fare.

A neighborhood specialty little known beyond Chicago's South Side is Atomic Cake. At least four local bakeries still create the 1950s-era multilayer delicacy with layers of whipped cream, chocolate ganache, chocolate cake, strawberry filling, strawberries, yellow cake, bananas, banana cream, and banana cake. A birthday delicacy, its recipe and history are murky, as is the origin of its name.

America's food icon, the Twinkie

Chicago's snack cake goes national

The Twinkie was created in Chicago. The filled sponge cake treat has become a cultural icon, an all-American snack.

In 1930, James Dewar of suburban Schiller Park, a manager at Continental Baking Company's Hostess Bakery, invented the Twinkie. At first, a banana cream–filled cake was created, a product that could use the shortbread pans that went idle when the strawberry shortcake season ended. During World War II, with imported bananas unavailable, the company switched to vanilla cream, and today's Twinkie was born. Dewar came up with the name after seeing a sign advertising Twinkle Toe Shoes.

A 1950s sponsor of TV's *Howdy Doody Show*, Twinkies were embraced by youngsters and became an American lunchbox favorite. Twinkies also became part of pop culture: When an accused murderer testified that he suffered from diminished capacity because he'd eaten too many snack cakes, his plea was dubbed "the Twinkie defense" and became a national joke.

 FOOD AND DRINK

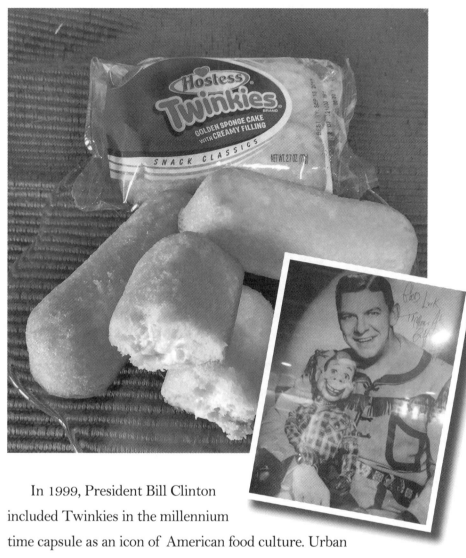

In 1999, President Bill Clinton included Twinkies in the millennium time capsule as an icon of American food culture. Urban legend has it that Twinkies will never get stale—that they have decades of shelf life—and Twinkies are used in creative ways: deep-fried at state fairs, to build wedding cakes, and even in sushi recipes offered by the company.

When Hostess Brands filed for bankruptcy in 2012, Twinkies vanished, and their fans were outraged. To cheers across the nation, the snack food returned to grocery stores the following year when Hostess was purchased out of bankruptcy.

"Cheezborger, cheezborger, cheezborger ... cheeps ... no Pepsi ... Coke"

Billy Goat Tavern

Immortalized by John Belushi, who portrayed a cranky Greek short-order cook on *Saturday Night Live*, the Billy Goat Tavern serves cheeseburgers, with no French fries—only chips and soda at its down-under location on Lower Michigan Avenue.

The bar is named for William "Billy Goat" Sianis, who opened the first bar in the early 1940s. He named it after a lost goat that wandered in when he was starting up. Sianis himself

FOOD AND DRINK

is infamous for casting the "goat curse" on the Chicago Cubs in 1945.

The "Cheezborger, cheezborger, cheezborger . . . no Coke . . . Pepsi" (with the words Pepsi and Coke in reverse order) routine was made famous by *SNL* cast members Belushi and Bill Murray, two actors with Chicago ties. The sketch was modeled after Sam Sianis, "Billy Goat's" descendant. With TV exposure, the popularity of the joint grew. Today, a small chain of Billy Goats include a popular Navy Pier location as well as the Lower Michigan Avenue location that opened in 1964.

The Goat, as it is known, is popular with tourists and local journalists alike. The latter, who often gather there, are honored with a wall of photos dedicated to journalism heroes. Times may have changed, but the food and the "no-options attitude" continue.

Brewskies and breweries

Chicago is a beer town

Chicago's story is soaked in beer. Immigrants from Ireland and Germany arrived in the 1830s and '40s, bringing with them cultures that included beer drinking in bars, taverns, and beer gardens.

Early settlement was in the South Loop, where proximity to the Chicago River provided a key ingredient for breweries. The first opened in 1833, producing ales and porters. By the 1840s, the first brewery making German-style lager appeared alongside the river.

From the 1860s to 1900, brewing was a huge industry, marked by continual changes in processes, from the introduction of pasteurization to refrigeration and scientific brewing. In 1893, Pabst won its Blue Ribbon at the 1893 World's Fair. By 1900, Chicago had sixty breweries producing more than one hundred million gallons of beer a year.

But Prohibition changed all that, giving rise to the beer wars of the 1920s, when Al Capone's battles for sales territories earned Chicago its "Mob town" reputation.

 FOOD AND DRINK

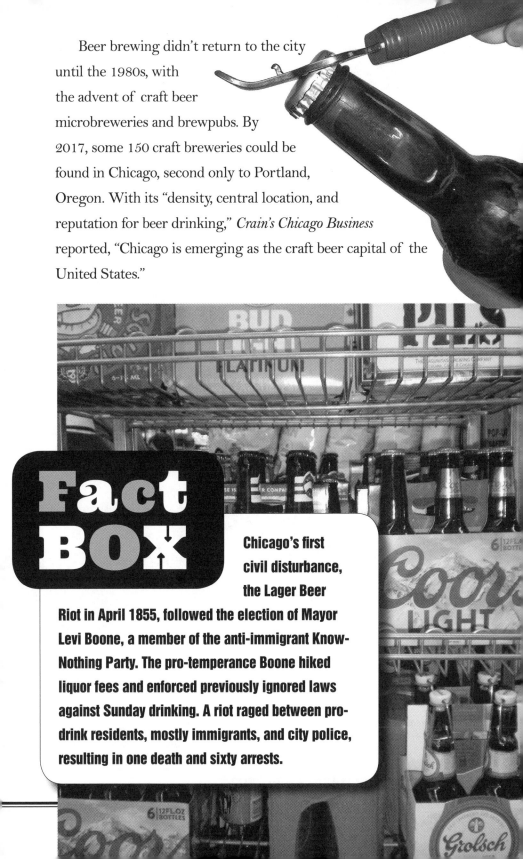

Beer brewing didn't return to the city until the 1980s, with the advent of craft beer microbreweries and brewpubs. By 2017, some 150 craft breweries could be found in Chicago, second only to Portland, Oregon. With its "density, central location, and reputation for beer drinking," *Crain's Chicago Business* reported, "Chicago is emerging as the craft beer capital of the United States."

Fact BOX

Chicago's first civil disturbance, the Lager Beer Riot in April 1855, followed the election of Mayor Levi Boone, a member of the anti-immigrant Know-Nothing Party. The pro-temperance Boone hiked liquor fees and enforced previously ignored laws against Sunday drinking. A riot raged between pro-drink residents, mostly immigrants, and city police, resulting in one death and sixty arrests.

Skoal!
It's Christmas
GLOGG

Drink up at Simon's Tavern

The neon sign hanging outside an Andersonville storefront sports a fish hoisting a martini glass. The fish is symbolic: It's a pickled herring.

It identifies Simon's Tavern, the last Swedish bar in this Scandinavian neighborhood. Simon's is known for its glogg, a concoction of port wine, brandy, oranges, raisins, sugar, and spices (cinnamon, ginger, cardamom, and cloves) served in a glass coffee mug with almonds and wine-soaked

EST. 1934

SWEA CHICAGO

FOOD AND DRINK

raisins. Glogg is the drink Swedes enjoy through the month-long festivities before Christmas. Other cultures call it "glow wine" because of the hot irons that mull the liquid.

Simon Lundberg came to the US in the early 1900s and became a citizen by fighting for his new country in World War I. He began business with a grocery store but turned to alcohol sales when he bought the bar in the 1930s, running a speakeasy out of the basement. He cashed employment checks for his patrons from the banklike safe in the corner and then retook the cash in payment for drink.

Simon's stayed in Lundberg's family through the mid-1990s, when new ownership took over, but the glogg continues to be popular, both during the winter and in summer, when Simon's serves it iced, as a slushy.

Fact BOX

Swedes left their mark on the North Side neighborhood called Andersonville. The commercial main drag, Clark Street, sports an eclectic mix of restaurants and bars alongside niche boutiques, the Swedish American Museum, and its Dala horse. Welcoming to families and a burgeoning LGBTQ community, Andersonville is among Chicago's most popular residential neighborhoods.

Soul food

from Chicago's South Side

Harold's Chicken Shack

In 1950, Harold Pierce, an African American entrepreneur, and his wife, Hilda, founded a restaurant called H&H on 39th Street, in the heart of Bronzeville, one of Chicago's original African American neighborhoods. At the time, many African Americans opened their own neighborhood shops, as the larger fast-food chains were reluctant to expand into black neighborhoods. In addition, African Americans found it hard to get the capital necessary for expansion beyond their own neighborhoods.

But Harold Pierce was persistent. The fried chicken restaurant he founded, now called Harold's Chicken Shack, became an expanding chain. Today, after Pierce's death, the company franchises operations, with locations in the city and suburban Chicago, Indiana, Detroit, Dallas, and Las Vegas.

FOOD AND DRINK

The eatery, also known as Harold's Chicken or simply Harold's, serves a half or quarter of a chicken with French fries, white bread, and coleslaw. Choices are all-white meat, all-dark meat, or a mix; the latter is ordered most. Prepared soul-food style, the chicken is fried in a mix of beef tallow and vegetable oil, and the final frying isn't done until an order is taken. The chain maintains these two factors create a dish akin to fried chicken from the Deep South.

The chicken dinner is the only consistent element at Harold's. Unlike national franchises that tout their similarities, Harold's lauds individuality: Some of the restaurants offer only carry-out, others are eat-in, and the menus offer different food and drink choices, but there is one constant: the logo of the cook chasing a chicken with a cleaver.

Che-cau-gou: the river is why we're here

The Chicago River, running through the city and to its north and south, is key to Chicago's development. Originally a meandering stream, it didn't have enough strength to power a water wheel, but it was the reason Chicago was settled.

When French voyageurs Father Jacques Marquette and Louis Joliet arrived in North America in 1673 seeking a direct trade route from New France/Canada to the Gulf of Mexico, Native Americans revealed the route from the Great Lakes to the Mississippi by the stream, other rivers, and a portage, a land strip where canoes and cargo were carried on the heads of traders. In 1848, when the Illinois and Michigan Canal opened, shipping exploded. Trade flourished, with the river acting as the main highway.

Indirectly, the river also gave Chicago its name. Native Americans called a wild garlic or skunk weed that grew along the river banks *checaugou*, but the word has also been translated as "something great," and Chicagoans prefer that definition.

 THE RIVER AND THE LAKE

The first permanent settler, in 1779, was Jean Baptiste Point DuSable, a Haitian with African ancestry, who opened a trading post at what was then the mouth of the river, land today under the Michigan Avenue bridge. Settlement increased, with industrial buildings and warehouses erected along the river, and vessels, ranging from freight steamships to excursion boats, crowded along the landings. In the twentieth century, when moving freight by water declined, the river became more of a recreational highway, with cruise boats, kayaks, and canoes.

Fact BOX

Originally, Chicago dumped waste into the Chicago River, which drained into Lake Michigan. As the lake was the city's drinking water source, disease spread. A decades-long project, the Sanitary and Ship Canal, reversed the river's flow in 1900, sending water and waste westward to the Mississippi River. It was the nation's largest municipal project of its time.

Ahoy there

Navy Pier

Navy Pier, or the People's Pier, as architect Daniel Burnham called it, is one of the city's most popular attractions. A record 9.3 million guests visited in 2016.

The Pier, which juts five-eighths of a mile into the lake, was built to implement Burnham's *1909 Plan of Chicago.* Though the plan envisioned five piers, Municipal Pier #2, as Navy Pier was originally known, was the only one built. The pier served steamship and freight traffic when it opened in 1916, but within a year, a public pier with entertainment, music, and restaurants was opened alongside the freight site.

Over the years, Navy Pier morphed into Army barracks for World War I soldiers, a training facility for World War II Navy pilots, and from 1945 to the late 1950s, the home to "Harvard on the Rocks," the University of Illinois' two-year college program for returning veterans.

 THE RIVER AND THE LAKE

In the 1970s, the pier reemerged as an entertainment venue when Mayor Michael Bilandic staged Chicago Fest, precursor to today's annual Taste of Chicago, on the site. In 1995, the pier was enclosed, and restaurants, movie theaters, the Chicago Shakespeare Theater, and the Chicago Children's Museum settled in along with the city's Ferris wheel.

In 2017, the Pier underwent yet more change with widened docks, additional restaurants and seating areas, and The Yard, a new venue for the Chicago Shakespeare Theater.

It's a green river

Almost everyone in Chicago is Irish on St. Patrick's Day. They prove it by dressing in shamrock green and gathering early in crowds along the Chicago River to watch city workers dye the river green. They follow up by standing for hours to watch the annual midday St. Patrick's Day Parade and then end up at pubs across the region to continue the celebration.

The Irish immigrated to the US in large numbers starting in the 1840s, first fleeing the potato famine and then following relatives who had found jobs here. Chicago's Irish are known for working in three segments of city life: police, priesthood, and politics. The active Irish community, in the South Side's Bridgeport and Canaryville neighborhoods, has produced twelve Chicago mayors and

 THE RIVER AND THE LAKE

innumerable aldermen and judges over the years.

The green river tradition began in 1961. That year's parade chairman, Stephen Bailey, noticed that the orange dye city workers used to detect waste in the river changed the water's color to emerald green. The powder's exact formula is top secret to this day. Dye is dumped into the river from one boat, while other boats zip behind to mix it into the water.

As green-clad celebrants cheer from the shore, the boats chase to and fro, shooting streams of green water high into the air.

Seesawing on the Chicago River

With the river running through it, it's not surprising that Chicago boasts many bridges. Of those, most are movable, the majority of them trunnion bascule seesaws.

From its inception, the city shipped freight along the river, whose banks were lined with warehouses and factories. A variety of bridge types was used throughout the nineteenth century: first drawbridges or floating bridges (rafts); followed by swing bridges, which rotated on piers so that boats could pass on either side; jackknife bridges, which rotated on a single pivot on or near the riverbank; and Scherzer rolling lift bridges, which opened by rolling back on a rocker.

Beginning in 1900, the city employed a new technology: trunnion bascule (French for "seesaw") bridges. The bridge, suspended

THE RIVER AND THE LAKE

on axles, or trunnions, is balanced by counterweights, opening with a motion similar to that of a playground seesaw. When the heavy counterweight drops, the bridge rises, and when the bridge is down, the counterweight is up. Chicago engineers modified and perfected the style, so much so that the bridges today are called "Chicago style."

In 1920, the first double-deck bridge was constructed, at Michigan Avenue. The Wells and Lake streets bridges also provide a second level for "L" tracks. Bridges over the river open on a set schedule, allowing tall-masted boats to get to and from the lake, mostly in the spring and fall.

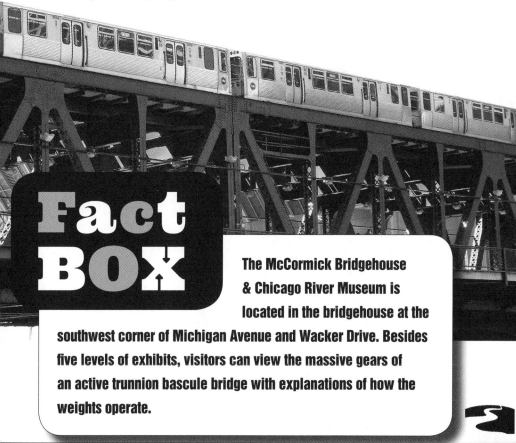

Fact BOX

The McCormick Bridgehouse & Chicago River Museum is located in the bridgehouse at the southwest corner of Michigan Avenue and Wacker Drive. Besides five levels of exhibits, visitors can view the massive gears of an active trunnion bascule bridge with explanations of how the weights operate.

Chicago's second coastline

CHICAGO RIVERWALK

likes th

Welcome to the Riverwalk

Since the mid-twentieth century, the Chicago River has been transformed into a recreational highway. Canoes, kayaks, and water taxis now share the water with cruise boats, personal pleasure boats, and the few barges left from the river's freight-highway past. Overlooking the banks are myriad high-rise offices, hotels, and residential buildings.

The Riverwalk, stretching 1.25 miles along the south bank from Lake Michigan to Lake Street, is filled with restaurants and bars, floating gardens, fountains, fishing piers, and sitting areas. Called

 THE RIVER AND THE LAKE

"an urban oasis in the heart of the city," the Riverwalk sits in part on landfill that was extended into the river.

The city-owned Riverwalk, which Mayor Rahm Emanuel calls the city's "second coastline," was completed in 2016. Reclaimed from formerly unused land along the river and built with walkways under the bridges, it is a unique urban park setting, designed for walking, strolling, sitting, and taking in the sights.

Fact BOX

The Riverwalk is part of the city's second wave of architectural landscaping; the first was creating parks in the late 1890s. The new wave began with Millennium Park and includes Maggie Daley Park and The 606 recreational trail. Also called "playful parks," these urban settings feature outdoor interactive activities and sustainable plantings.

The Riverwalk is divided into six "rooms," spaces beneath and between the bridges, each with its own name and function: Marina, Cove, River Theater, Water Plaza, Jetty, and Riverbank. Two are aimed specifically at children: Water Plaza, with an interactive fountain, and Jetty, where fishing and fish breeding will be central to ecology classes. The other rooms offer docking space for boats and outdoor dining with diverse food offerings.

Chicago's "inland sea"

When visitors to Chicago first see Lake Michigan, many exclaim, "It's an ocean!" because water is all that's visible on the eastern horizon, but though it's often called an inland sea, Lake Michigan is indeed a lake: one of the largest freshwater lakes in the country and the only one of the Great Lakes without a Canadian shore. Thirty miles of its shoreline are in Chicago, all but four of them publicly owned.

The lakefront is Chicago's front yard, offering miles of green space and recreation. "Chicago today has one of the most magnificent waterfronts in the world," wrote Donald L. Miller in *City of the Century*. Its chain of sandy beaches, curving trails, and parks both large and small are enjoyed by sunbathers and swimmers, bicyclists, rollerbladers, joggers, and walkers. The swath of green evolved from the 1837 incorporation map of Chicago that showed the land open and free, followed by architect and planner Daniel Burnham's pledge, in his *1909 Plan of Chicago*, to give citizens one great unobstructed lakefront view by relocating the city's freight facilities elsewhere.

 THE RIVER AND THE LAKE

Lake Michigan is vital to the city's well-being. In addition to providing Chicagoans' drinking water, the lake offers extensive opportunities for fishing and boating. In the warm months of the year, its many harbors and marinas are filled with both sailing and motor boats.

"We don't want nobody NOBODY sent."

Chicago is known for politics, specifically, a Democratic Party machine that runs the city through clout and patronage. That machine was created by Mayor Anton Cermak in the 1930s, combining various immigrant and working-class voters, and has functioned well ever since, giving Democrats city control year after year.

Machine politics, which means strict adherence to the party's directives, including voting for the party's nominees for offices up and down the ballot, most famously has been credited with the presidential election of John F. Kennedy in 1960.

The invocation "We don't want nobody . . ." comes from a story the late Judge Abner Mikva told of trying to volunteer for the 1948 gubernatorial campaign of Adlai Stevenson. When asked

 POLITICS, CHICAGO STYLE

who had sent him, Mikva replied, "Nobody sent me," to which the ward politician responded, "We don't want nobody nobody sent." No political sponsor? No need to apply for a political job. Milton Rakove, a University of Illinois at Chicago professor, is incorrectly given credit for the famous line when he featured the practice in his book *We Don't Want Nobody Nobody Sent.*

According to author Adam Selzer (*Chronicles of Old*

Chicago), it's "the preferred way to encapsulate the classic Chicago political machine," emphasizing the city's reputation for cronyism and the notion that political connections, not qualifications, are what's needed to get a government job.

"Chicago way"

Chicago politics was likely corrupt from the beginning, but practices were elevated to an art in the early twentieth century by two corrupt aldermen, Michael "Hinky Dink" Kenna and "Bathhouse" John Coughlin, of the notorious First Ward, which was then a lower-class West Side neighborhood.

Each of the city's ward aldermen had local power equivalent to that of a mayor. Beginning in the late nineteenth century, the First Ward was the city's center of corruption. Aldermen bought votes with gift turkeys and provided city jobs to the unqualified, ruling their domains through zoning changes in exchange for bribes, ignoring crime in return for payments, and favoring specific businesses.

The First Ward was also known for crime, with flourishing brothels, beer businesses run by precursors to the Al Capone gang, and taverns with colorful names, such as The Bucket of Blood and Bed Bug Row. The two aldermen were also infamous for sponsoring what reformers called a "disgrace to Chicago": the First Ward

 POLITICS, CHICAGO STYLE

Words and Music
BY
JOHN J. COUGHLIN

Ball. The annual event, a huge party where alcohol flowed, was a get-rich quick scheme built on ticket and liquor sales.

Hinky Dink owned the Workingman's Exchange, a popular saloon. Bathhouse John, who got his moniker from working in a bathhouse, is remembered for writing songs, including "Dear Midnight of Love" and poetry often regarded as doggerel.

Largest city council in the country

Each ward runs like a small city

Chicago has a mayor-council form of government. The government's legislative branch, the Chicago City Council, consists of fifty aldermen elected from fifty wards, each serving a four-year term. The council makes the laws on taxes, utilities, and landmarking, among other issues. The mayor serves as presiding officer, and the city clerk is secretary; both are popularly elected. The city council meets, usually monthly, in city hall.

The division of the city into wards has been on the books since 1837, when Chicago was incorporated. Beginning with six, the system grew to fifty wards by 1923. Chicago is unique among major cities in the United States in the number of wards and aldermen it maintains. Although they're elected on a nonpartisan basis, almost all aldermen are Democrats. According to supporters, the system promotes diverse ethnic representation, but the city council has for years been at the center of Chicago's reputation for public corruption.

Between 1972 and 1999, twenty-six current or former Chicago

 POLITICS, CHICAGO STYLE

aldermen were convicted of official corruption. Between 1973 and 2012, a period during which approximately one hundred people served as aldermen, about one-third of them, thirty-one, were convicted of corruption.

Chicago aldermen have firm control over what happens in their wards. "Aldermanic privilege" allows each to make determinations regarding zoning, licenses, permits, city contracts, and patronage jobs. It's as if each alderman was the mayor of his ward, holding veto power concerning issues ranging from development to garbage collection to policing.

Chicago's BLACK political machine

From William L. Dawson to Harold Washington

While the tight-knit Irish community long controlled Chicago's Democratic machine, African American residents organized a "submachine" in five African American wards of Chicago. Working partners, whites and blacks separately secured votes from their own areas but combined forces on behalf of the Democratic citywide platform.

William L. Dawson was the most powerful African American politician in Chicago from 1942 until his death in 1970. He was a ward committeeman, congressman, and creator of the submachine, but following his death, disagreements arose between whites and blacks over three key issues: housing, schools, and police. Mayor Richard J. Daley could most often be found championing white voters' views, favoring segregated housing and schools, and upholding police actions.

After Daley's death in 1976, political instability opened the door to new voting patterns, and following a three-way 1983 primary, Harold Washington was elected the city's first African American mayor. The

 POLITICS, CHICAGO STYLE

election unleashed Chicago's racism, as the so-called "Council Wars" pitted the mayor against the "Vrdolyak 29," an all-white aldermanic majority bloc led by Edward "Fast Eddie" Vrdolyak and Edward Burke. For two years, city council action stalled. Appointments remained in limbo, and bills died. Often tumultuous meetings deteriorated into shouting matches, with aldermen jumping on their desks and ranting.

The Council Wars ended in May 1986 when a federal court ordered special elections in seven wards, remapped to reflect the growth of Chicago's African American and Hispanic populations. An African American, Eugene Sawyer, followed Washington with a two-year term, but since then Chicago hasn't elected another African American mayor.

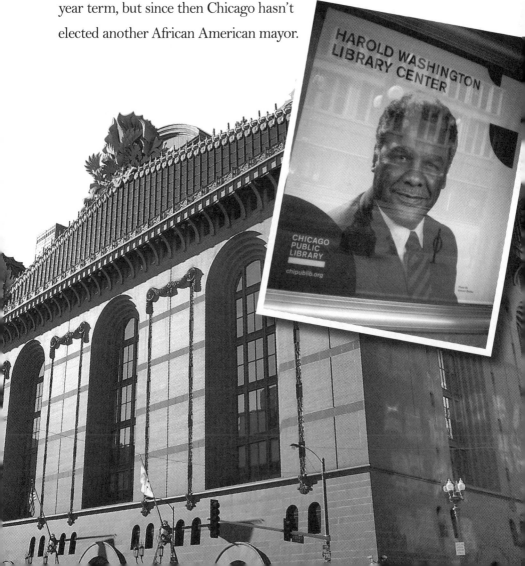

Chicago's salad bowl

City of ethnic neighborhoods

Cities like Chicago that have grown through immigration are often labeled a melting pot. In Chicago, though, a more appropriate term is "salad bowl," with each neighborhood individually identified like the vegetables in a salad, all tossed with the common Chicago dressing.

A precise tally of neighborhoods is elusive: One source says seventy-seven, while another claims two hundred. Seventy-seven is generally cited, and it's the number recognized by the city. Neighborhoods are grouped into nine areas, such as Far North Side, Northwest Side, or South Side. Strikingly, there is no East Side. The east has always been solely Lake Michigan, although a new downtown development, Lakeshore East, east of Michigan Avenue, is using the designation.

Many neighborhoods developed as immigrants flowed into the city and settled near one another. Pilsen was first settled by Bohemians and Czechs who named their neighborhood after a city in Bohemia. There's no mystery about the early residents of Little Italy, Greektown, and Chinatown, and Bridgeport and Canaryville were heavily populated by Irish immigrants and their

 POLITICS, CHICAGO STYLE

descendants. Andersonville was once a Swedish-Norwegian community. Some neighborhoods grew out of the city's unofficial segregation policy, one of which is Bronzeville, the South Side area to which deed covenants restricted African Americans.

Regardless of their origins, many of these neighborhoods vigorously express their identities with shops that specialize in imported goods, restaurants that serve ethnic foods, parades that herald ethnic or religious holidays, and in some areas murals or other street decor highlighting ethnic heritage.

Fact BOX

Chicago reinforces neighborhood identity by providing distinctive streetscapes that highlight locations. In Chinatown, dragons perch on light poles; in Pilsen, a Mexican American area, light poles hold metal eagles gripping a snake, symbols from Mexico's flag. In Boystown, which has a large LGBTQ population, a series of sand-colored columns sport rainbow bands of the LGBTQ flag.

"We ain't ready for reform."

Chicago's political machine

The last Republican mayor of Chicago was William "Big Bill" Thompson, who was elected three times between 1915 and 1931. He was defeated by Anton Cermak, the first immigrant to hold the office and the father of the modern Democratic machine that still influences Chicago politics.

When Cermak died after two years in office, two party officials, Cook County Democratic Chairman Patrick Nash and sanitary district official Edward Kelly, took control. Kelly was elected mayor, and the so-called Kelly-Nash machine maintained power until 1947.

POLITICS, CHICAGO STYLE

A political machine secures votes through offers of patronage jobs and services. Using ward committeemen to choose candidates for backing in primaries, supervise precinct captains, and administer elections, the Kelly-Nash and later the Richard J. Daley machine kept Democrats in power. Daley became one of the strongest Democratic mayors in city history, from his 1955 election until his death in 1976.

Machine operations floundered over the next thirteen years under five different mayors. When Richard J.'s son, Richard M. Daley, was elected mayor in 1989, a more traditional Democrat took the reins again, although the machine had been weakened.

Along with ensuring the election of Democratic mayors for decades, the machine has also brought political corruption to the body politic in the form of patronage jobs, bribery, and favoritism— and Chicagoans know that. They've long been familiar with how the system works. It's almost as if politics has been a spectator sport, writes historian Robin Einhorn, and as Alderman "Paddy" Bauler proclaimed in 1955, "Chicago ain't ready for reform."

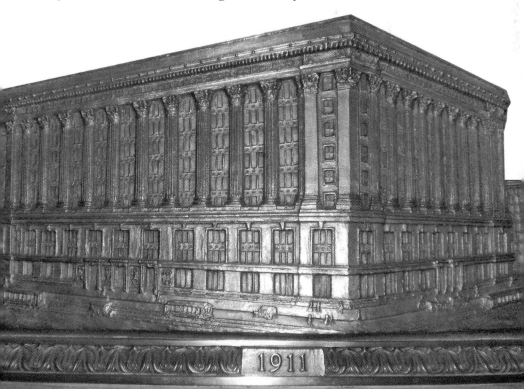

1911

How do you say it: CHEE-CAW-GO or CHEE-CAH-GO?

What accent?

"Accents are an important element of regional identity. And an important element of Midwestern identity is believing you don't have an accent—that you speak a neutral brand of standardized English," says linguist Edward McClelland.

Chicagoans accept that. They think they have no accent, but some outsiders do hear an accent here, one with pronunciations closer to those of Buffalo residents than to fellow Midwesterners. That's because Chicago is in what McClelland calls the Inland North, the lower Great Lakes region that extends from Buffalo to Milwaukee.

The Inland North was settled primarily by New Englanders in the early nineteenth century, and they brought their speech patterns along with their investments, entrepreneurship, and settlements. The exact speech pattern is a result of what McClelland calls the Northern Cities Vowel Shift or what other linguists call "*a* raising." Simply put, it's the reason that Chicagoans say *cayen* for "can," *bahhx* for "box," and *suvun* for "seven."

 WHADDAYA MEAN?

Another major influence on Chicago speech was television. By the 1950s, when TV was young and many shows originated in the city, reportorial accents had changed. The pre-World War II, New England-accented, upper-class English of Franklin Roosevelt and Lowell Thomas was replaced by speech patterns without accented r's. That flattened speech became Chicago's and the nation's standard.

Fact BOX

African Americans came to Chicago in large numbers in what's known as the Great Migration, the movement of African Americans north between 1915 and 1975. Edward McClelland notes that these newcomers to the city were isolated in separate neighborhoods by the racist policies of the time, and, as a result, retained their native Southern speech patterns.

Fans, coach call them "Da Bears"

Celebrating Chicago's working class

The official name of Chicago's National Football League team is the Chicago Bears. Originally the Decatur Staleys, they became the Bears in 1922, but since winning the Super Bowl in 1986, the team has reveled in the nickname that reflects the city's working-class persona.

"Da Bears," which affectionately mocks Chicago-inflected "dese, dems, and dose" speech, was popularized by a recurring skit on *Saturday Night Live* that featured players who were connected to Chicago in one way or another: Joe Mantegna, Mike Myers, Chris Farley, and Kevin Nealon. As locals who were members of "Bill Swerski's Super Fans" club, they delivered Chicagoese lines like "You gonna watch da game?" and "Whataya, stupid?"

The satire also echoed the speech patterns of the winning Bears team's head coach, Mike Ditka, a standout Bears player before he turned to coaching. It was Ditka who invented "Grabowski," the blue-collar, lunch-bucket laborer who was said to be the iconic 1985 Bears fan.

 WHADDAYA MEAN?

Ditka parlayed his mid-'80s fame into an eponymous steakhouse chain and a string of product endorsement ads in which he usually appears wearing a sweater vest in blue and orange team colors with "Bears" emblazoned on the front.

"Meet under the clock"
and other familiar phrases

If a Chicago friend said you'd "meet under the clock," you would've known to head to State Street to await her arrival under one of two big clocks attached to what was the busiest and most successful department store there, Marshall Field's. The phrase was a quick appointment to get together downtown, and it's still heard today, even though the department store there is now Macy's.

Chicago's criminal associations and political and social history have given rise to other phrases that are used far beyond the city.

One is "smoke-filled room," originally referring to a Blackstone Hotel suite where GOP politicos met during their 1920 national convention to select Warren G. Harding as their presidential nominee because the floor vote had deadlocked. Now the phrase indicates any political activity occurring out of the public eye.

 WHADDAYA MEAN?

"Public enemy" also originated in Chicago, when the Chicago Crime Commission under director Henry Barrett Chamberlain used it in 1931 for a list of twenty-eight gangsters. The list, a publicity move to arouse the public, was topped by Al Capone, Public Enemy #1.

Finally, "the midway" now denotes the amusement area of carnivals and fairs around the world, but the name was originally a reference to the Midway Plaisance, where the less formal exhibits and amusement park rides and shows were located during the 1893 World's Columbian Exposition.

We just *blew* in

Though the city has many nicknames, the one heard most often is "Windy City."

Ask the tourists being buffeted by the wind off Lake Michigan and they'll readily agree that it's apt, perhaps noting that Chicago's wind not only exists but can also be brutal. The name fits the climate.

In truth, though, the title doesn't refer to the wind. Rather, it refers to Chicago's braggadocio.

According to many authors, Chicago's lobbyists were vigorous in proclaiming the city's virtues when trying to persuade Congress to choose Chicago to host what was to be the 1892 World's Fair, and they were tagged as braggarts. Chicago's efforts prompted *New York*

 WHADDAYA MEAN?

54

Sun Editor Charles A. Dana to write: "Don't pay attention to the nonsensical claims of that windy city. Its people could not build a world's fair even if they won it."

Other modern historians dispute whether Dana was actually the writer of that quote, but no one doubts it was the city's bragging that evoked the nickname. Whatever the circumstances, Chicago has embraced the moniker; in fact, the wind is immortalized in ornamentation on the Harold Washington Library Center.

Perhaps Dana was right: The fair was indeed built by Chicago, but it opened a year late.

Fact BOX

One nickname never embraced was "Mudhole on the Prairie." In its early days, the city was viewed as wild, uncultured, and scrappy. To dispel this perception, city fathers showed off at the 1893 World's Columbian Exposition with a new opera house, top-drawer hotels, and a fast-growing collection of skyscrapers. "Mudhole" wasn't heard again.

Which title really says "Chicago"?

Nicknames and slogans abound for Chicago. Each comes from a different era, reflecting the city at the time it was bestowed.

Urbs in horto, or City in a Garden, was the name Chicago gave itself in 1837 when it incorporated. It was an unlikely name, as the city had few gardens then, and marsh and mud were typical, but city fathers encouraged the planting of gardens to highlight the city's refinement and culture. Today, boosters of new sites, such as Millennium and Maggie Daley parks, the Riverwalk, and The 606 recreational trail, use the nickname's spirit to guide development.

Other less formal names similarly reflect history. Hog Butcher to the World, poet Carl Sandburg's tribute, rose from the phenomenal success of the stockyards, the center of the nation's meat packing and processing industry until the mid-twentieth century. The name stressed the working-class nature of the city—the manual laborers who toiled in its manufacturing enterprises.

 WHADDAYA MEAN?

The City That Works was a double-edged nickname, arising during the era of Mayor Richard J. Daley, from 1955 to 1976. On the one hand, Daley ran an efficient city, providing necessary services, such as garbage collection and police and fire protection, but his autocratic rule was backed by machine politics, patronage, and suppression of dissent, giving the name an ironic twist.

And Second City? It was written by *New Yorker* writer A. J. Liebling as a sneer at Chicago's loss in population, but it is celebrated as Chicago's spirit, embraced with humor by the eponymous comedy club.

Urbs in horto

Ubi est mea?

HOG BUTCHER TO THE WORLD

THE CITY THAT WORKS

Second City

Early dynasty to Lovable Losers

The Chicago Cubs

Chicago's much-loved baseball team, the Cubs, dates to 1876 and is the only founding National League franchise still playing in its original city. Originally known as the White Stockings, the team won the first National League Championship and became one of baseball's early dynasties, winning six of the first eleven championships from 1876 to 1886. For some years they played on Chicago's West Side.

The modern-day Cubs date to 1903. A record 116 wins in 1906 brought the team its first pennant, but it lost the World Series to the crosstown rival White Sox in the first series to feature same-city teams. In the next two years, the Cubs became the first team to win back-to-back World Series.

WEST SIDE GROUNDS
HOME FIELD OF THE CHICAGO NATIONAL LEAGUE BALL C
FROM 1893 TO 1915

SEATING CAPACITY: 16,000
FIRST GAME: MAY 14, 1893 (CINCINNATI 13, CHICAGO 12)
LAST GAME: OCTOBER 3, 1915 (CHICAGO 7, ST. LOUIS 2)
CAREER RECORD AT WEST SIDE GROUNDS: 1,018 WINS, 640 LOSSES
WORLD SERIES CHAMPIONS: 1907, 1908
NATIONAL LEAGUE CHAMPIONS: 1906,1907,1908,1910

SPORTS

From 1876 to 1945, the Chicago Cubs was one of the most successful baseball teams in the country, posting a 5,475-4,324 (.559) record with fifty-one winning seasons. That ended with the 1945 World Series loss to the Detroit Tigers.

For the next twenty years, the Cubs would finish each season at fifth place or lower, inspiring the "Lovable Losers" moniker and the "Wait 'til next year" lament. Not until 2016 did the Cubs finally win the World Series again, ending a 108-year drought. Lovable losing was over.

Fact BOX

William "Billy Goat" Sianis bought 1945 World Series tickets for himself and his goat, Murphy. The goat wasn't allowed in. Sianis asked why. Cubs owner P.K. Wrigley said: "Because the goat stinks." Sianis retaliated with a curse: "The Cubs will never win a World Series so long as the goat is not allowed in Wrigley Field." When the Cubs lost, Sianis sent another message: "Who stinks now?" The curse wasn't broken until 2016, when the Cubs finally won the series.

Friendly confines:
Wrigley Field

Cubs at home in Rickettsville

Chicagoans cherish Wrigley Field. Throughout decades of their team's mediocre play, Chicago Cubs fans loyally turned out to enjoy the wind blowing over Waveland Avenue (a notorious enabler of home runs), the ivy on the walls, inexpensive bleacher seats, popcorn, and hot dogs in the "friendly confines." The name was popularized by "Mr. Cub," Ernie Banks, shortstop and first baseman from 1953 to 1971.

The 1914 stadium was originally Weeghman Park, named for the owner of the Federal League Chicago Whales. The Whales lasted only one year, but the stadium kept the name, even after the Chicago Cubs, a Major League team, moved in in 1916.

"LET'S PLAY TWO"

ERNIE BANKS
"MR. CUB"

SPORTS

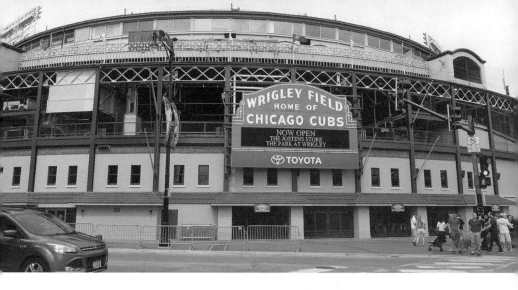

Chewing gum magnate William Wrigley Jr. took control of the Cubs in 1921, and the field was called Cubs Park until 1926, when it was renamed. Today, it stands as the oldest park in the National League and second oldest in the majors after Boston's Fenway Park, which dates to 1912.

A massive redevelopment of Wrigley Field and its site is ongoing, transforming the neighborhood into what some derisively call "Rickettsville," after the Cubs' current owner-family. The five-year, $750 million redevelopment includes a hotel, shopping center-open air plaza dubbed The Park at Wrigley, a new 30,000-square-foot clubhouse, added corporate luxury boxes, a VIP Experience club, a six-story office building for Cubs administrative offices, and more. Although some critics look askance at the changes, accusing the Ricketts of bringing "suburbanism" to the city, most fans still think of Wrigley as the friendly confines.

The Bears: Monsters of the Midway

Chicago's professional football team

The Decatur Staleys, a company team formed in 1919 by the A. E. Staley food starch company of Decatur, Illinois, within a year came under the control of football genius George "Papa Bear" Halas. He moved the team to Chicago and in 1922 renamed it "Bears" in a nod to baseball's Chicago Cubs, who hosted the football team at their stadium.

In its long history, the Bears have captured nine National Football League championships, notched one Super Bowl victory, in 1986, and recorded more wins and placed more team members (27) in the Pro Football Hall of Fame than any other franchise.

In the early twentieth century, the Bears were a powerhouse, appropriating the nickname Monsters of the Midway, a term first used for the University of Chicago's Big Ten football team. Among his accomplishments, Halas created a new approach to offense, the T-formation, setting the stage for modern football.

With the increasing popularity of pro football, the NFL required team stadiums to seat at least fifty thousand. For that and other reasons, the Bears in 1971 moved from their North Side home of fifty years to Soldier Field on the Near South Side. Along with a new stadium, the team set out to become a Super Bowl champion, which coach Mike Ditka finally achieved in 1986.

Since then, despite high hopes at the start of each season, fans have invariably been disappointed. In 2015, the Bears hired a new head coach. Though things didn't improve in 2016-17, residents always look ahead to next season.

White Sox, Black Sox

The Chicago White Sox

Charles Comiskey owned the White Sox baseball team, which joined the American League in 1900. Within a decade, the Sox settled into a stadium at 35th Street and Shields Avenue on the city's South Side. Comiskey, for whom the ballpark was named, was a shrewd manager and a notoriously parsimonious owner, paying low salaries, few if any bonuses, and even requiring team members to launder their own uniforms.

By 1918, Comiskey had signed enough well-known ball players, including Joseph Jefferson, "Shoeless" Joe Jackson, pitcher Ed Cicotte, first baseman "Chick" Gandil, and shortstop "Swede" Risberg, to create what was expected to be a winning dynasty.

But the next year, when the White Sox won the American League pennant and were favored to beat the Cincinnati Reds in the World Series, they unexpectedly lost. An ensuing investigation

SPORTS

Joe Jackson, called "Shoeless" after he played a minor league game in his stocking feet because new shoes didn't fit, came to the White Sox in 1915. In 1919, he batted .351 in the regular season and .375 with perfect fielding during the Series, but the team lost. He and seven teammates were accused of throwing the series. Despite his protestations and the findings of a Chicago jury that he was not involved, Jackson, like the others, was banned from baseball.

uncovered the scandal of the "Black Sox"—players who had allegedly conspired with gamblers to throw at least two of the games.

In August 1921, Major League Baseball Commissioner Kennesaw Mountain Landis, a former federal judge, banned eight implicated players from baseball for life. The Black Sox scandal reverberated throughout the sporting world and left Comiskey a broken man. Under his ownership, the team never won another pennant or World Series.

Bulls, Blackhawks, Sky, Fire, and Dogs

Chicago is a sports-happy town

There's no off-season in Chicago. The city revels in sports: at events, on the seemingly nonstop TV and radio sports shows, at team fan fests, and with ubiquitous logo-stamped merchandise. If there is a way to enjoy sports, Chicago does it, down to putting the headgear of championship teams on the heads of the Art Institute of Chicago's bronze lion statues.

Chicago, which has been named Best Sports City by *Sporting News* three times, in 1993, 2006, and 2010, boasts professional teams in all of the nation's major sports, one of only four US cities with that distinction.

Beyond cheering baseball's Cubs at Wrigley Field and Sox at Guaranteed Rate Field and football's Bears at Soldier Field, the crowds roar for the National Basketball Association's Bulls and the National Hockey League's Blackhawks, both of which play at the

SPORTS

United Center; Major League Soccer's Chicago Fire at Toyota Park; and the Women's National Basketball Association's Chicago Sky at the Allstate Arena.

Chicagoans haven't forgotten Stanley Cup-winning hockey from the Blackhawks in 2015, 2013, and 2010 or the remarkable six Bulls championships in the 1990s Michael Jordan and Scottie Pippen era.

For those who crave baseball, there are also minor league teams, including the newest, the Chicago Dogs of the American Association of Independent Professional Baseball, that will open play in 2018 in northwest suburban Rosemont.

Other minor league, semipro, and amateur Chicago teams include the Chicago Lions and Chicago Griffins, rugby; the Chicago Wolves, an American Hockey League franchise; and the Windy City Rollers, roller derby players who skate at the University of Illinois at Chicago Pavilion.

Chicago's game:

16-inch softball

No mitts, slow pitch

Summer in Chicago begins when park district lights come on in the evenings and uniformed teams take to the fields to play Chicago's game: 16-inch softball. The large, soft ball makes for a slow-pitched game with good contact opportunities for the batter and allows the game to be played without mitts.

Softball was invented in Chicago in 1887. Creator George Hancock crafted a ball from boxing gloves with laces and used a broomstick as a bat. The first games were played indoors, but within a year, the teams moved outside. A ball with a sixteen-inch diameter proved perfect for Chicago's small parks and schoolyards.

Still, a fourteen-inch ball was used in 1933 when seventy thousand people saw the first major softball tournament at the city's Century of Progress Exposition. Across America today, softball players mostly use twelve-inch balls. While sixteen-inch softball remains almost exclusively Chicago's game, a similar "mushball" is played in Portland, Oregon.

 **SPORTS**

The Chicago Park District maintains 224 ball fields. Leagues are offered for all-male, all-female, or co-ed competitive or recreational softball teams. One league is solely for Chicago Public School students. The Chicago 16-Inch Softball Hall of Fame, formed to promote the game, opened in 2014 in Forest Park, a Chicago suburb.

Chicago leather plays in Super Bowl

Local firms supply footballs

SPORTS

Chicago's Bears have not appeared in a Super Bowl for more than three decades, but the city is represented every year. Chicago-based Wilson Sporting Goods provides Super Bowl footballs with leather crafted by Horween Leather Co.

A football, technically a prolate spheroid, is called a "pigskin." Early football games used a ball made from inflated pig bladders. Leather came later, the skin stitched together by laces. Today's balls still include laces but not for closure; players use the laces to grip the ball. Early balls were difficult to blow up, and their shapes varied. With leather balls, the shape became more consistent, but the ends became more pronounced when the game embraced the forward pass.

Wilson's is proud that "every throw, every kick, every touchdown, and every point in every NFL game has been with a Wilson football," as the company proclaims in its advertising, and Horween Leather is equally proud. While Horween provides leather for Spaulding basketballs and Rawlings baseball gloves, it does most of its 40 percent sports work for footballs. Horween, founded in 1905, began tanning footballs in the 1940s, when Horween's teamed up with Wilson and George Halas to make a better ball, according to Nick Horween, part of the family-owned company's fifth generation.

Horween Leather tans steer hides, which are treated to remove fats and oil, and adds chrome salts for strength. Horween, in an interview with the *Chicago Tribune*, explained that football leather has a grippable tackiness, which is "part of the reason (he) is irked when announcers blame flubbed passes on slippery balls."

World's busiest or world's worst?

O'Hare International Airport

Opened in 1955, Chicago's O'Hare International sits high on the list of the world's busiest airports. It also is found at or near the top on a list of the world's worst. The airport is tethered to Chicago by a strip of land just two hundred feet wide, a connection that allows the city to control the facility and benefit economically from its taxes and business activity.

The airport is named for Edward "Butch" O'Hare, a Chicago World War II hero. In 1942, he single-handedly shot down five Japanese planes, for which he received the Congressional Medal of Honor. O'Hare was killed in 1943, and the city renamed its then "out-of-the-way" airport in his

 TO AND FRO, TRANSPORTATION

honor. The name replaced the site's former moniker, Orchard Field, but the airport still uses ORD as its symbol.

O'Hare is dubbed "worst" because of its long walkways and long waits. With 182 gates in four terminals and two main cargo areas, the airport has gone without a facelift or addition since 2013. Plans are now under way for interior space upgrades in an effort to improve its competitive position.

In 2016, O'Hare accounted for nearly 20 percent of flight cancellations across the country. Chicago's weather hinders tens of thousands of travelers annually, who become stranded waiting for storms to clear, snow to stop, or a plane to be de-iced.

O'Hare by the numbers:
In 2016, O'Hare welcomed over seventy-seven million passengers and 1.7 million metric tons of cargo. In 2017, flights served 208 destinations, 153 of them domestic and 55 international. A major hub for both American and United airlines, the airport was the United States' third busiest and the sixth busiest in the world.

Riding the rails

Railroad center of the nation

Almost since the first train steamed into Chicago from Galena,
Illinois, in the 1850s, the city has been the center of the nation's
railroad network, owing in part to its location in the middle of
the country. It is often joked that freight takes six days to cross
the continent: two days from the East Coast to Chicago, two days
from the West Coast to Chicago, and two days switching around
in Chicago.

Today, more lines of track can be found in Chicago than in any
other North American city. Besides the freight-only lines, there are
the routes of Amtrak, the national passenger line, and Metra, the
area's publicly owned suburban commuter rail system, which runs on
freight-railroad owned tracks.

The city became crisscrossed with tracks in the late nineteenth
century. Even in the post-World War II years, when more freight
began moving by plane and truck, the city's relationship with
railroads was evident in the numerous rail viaducts, overpasses, and
street-level crossings where trains still travel.

TO AND FRO, TRANSPORTATION

The railroads played a role in Chicago's love affair with the skyscraper, as several prominent postwar buildings stand on air rights over tracks. Among them are the Prudential Center and the Boeing Building. Even Millennium Park, Chicago's favorite downtown park, is a green roof constructed over still-active railroad tracks.

Fact BOX

In the nineteenth century, prominent Illinois politicians often had railroad connections. US Senator Stephen Douglas lobbied to make Chicago the nation's rail hub, aware that railroads would have to purchase right-of-way land he had to sell, and his pre-Civil War era rival, Abraham Lincoln, before he was president, was a lawyer for the Illinois Central Railroad.

The "L":
"world's best urban gondola ride"

Chicago's elevated transit system

Chicago is the only major American city still sporting a downtown elevated transit system. Dating from the 1890s, Chicago's "L" makes a loop around the downtown business district before spreading out along five lines to the boundaries of the city and beyond.

The first "L" was built heading south from downtown and then extended to serve the 1893 World's Fair. The downtown tracks running in an oval around the city's center were developed by Charles Tyson Yerkes, a Philadelphia robber baron who bribed and conned his way through Chicago politics to get it built.

TO AND FRO, TRANSPORTATION

Transformed into a public transit system in the late 1940s, the Loop "L" was saved from demolition in the 1970s by preservationists who touted its importance in the city's history. In 2016, the system carried 238.6 million passengers, the second-highest annual level in its history.

As author Tom Chiarella, who dubbed the "L" an urban gondola ride, wrote, "The 'L' is the best mass transit system in the United States. Not the fastest, nor the most reliable. Not the newest, nor the longest. The best." Why? Because seated anywhere from twenty to thirty feet above the ground, riders enjoy exquisite views of the city. The unique experience is also the least expensive way to see the city.

Fact BOX

The Loop's "L" train tracks overlook the city's downtown, an oval system that dates to 1897. The term "loop," however, predates that system. "Loop" referred to the route of city streetcars that circled the business district. The trains' loop emphasized that area and gave Chicago's downtown its name.

Expressways, not freeways; names, not numbers

Chicago's Interstate Highway System

Chicago visitors often find it difficult to follow local driving directions. While elsewhere in the country, Eisenhower-era Interstate Highway System roads are called "freeways," in Chicago they're "expressways." To make it more difficult, Chicagoans don't refer to them by their interstate route numbers, such as I-290 or I-294, two major routes. Rather, each road has a name, usually that of a local politician. Being Chicago, the named pols are mostly Democrats, with Presidents Dwight Eisenhower and Ronald Reagan Republican exceptions.

The network of superhighways and toll roads was built in a hub-and-spoke pattern, radiating from the center of the city in all directions, allowing for fast entry

TO AND FRO, TRANSPORTATION

to downtown. It also offered many people the opportunity to move to the suburbs.

The first expressway built was the Eisenhower, an expansion of the former Congress Parkway to six lanes. Having such a road was envisioned in architect Daniel Burnham's *1909 Plan of Chicago*, although it wasn't built until 1955. The route runs spectacularly through what once was the city's gigantic main post office.

From that beginning, additional expressways were dedicated through the 1950s and 1960s. Most recently, an interchange of four expressways, previously known as the Circle, was renamed for former Mayor Jane Byrne. She, too, of course, was a Democrat.

Other than presidents, Chicago's expressways are named for Illinois politicians: I-55's Adlai Stevenson II was governor; I-94's Dan(iel) Ryan was Cook County Board president; and I-94's stretch to the north of downtown honors William G. Edens, the Illinois Bankers Association member who lobbied for the state's first highway bond legislation in 1918.

The spirit of "I Will"

The Water Tower

The Water Tower, the crenellated structure standing proud but no longer tall among its high-rise neighbors on North Michigan Avenue, is the embodiment of the city's motto: "I Will."

Built before the Great Chicago Fire of 1871, the water tower and companion pumping station were part of Chicago's early

effort to provide safe drinking water. The two buildings were connected to a tunnel stretching two miles out into Lake Michigan, where a "crib" drew fresh water, unpolluted by waste runoff into the lake from the Chicago River.

Designed by W.W. Boyington, one of Chicago's first architects, the Gothic-designed limestone buildings remind viewers of an

ONLY IN CHICAGO

English castle with its towers, turrets, and slit windows. The water tower hid a three-foot diameter, 140-foot-tall standpipe that secured the water pressure for the city's North Side.

The Water Tower became Chicago's symbol when it survived the Great Fire. It owed its survival partly to the water superintendent, who wrapped it in soaked sheets, in anticipation of the northward-moving flames. After the three-day blaze had burned out, the Water Tower and Pumping Station were among only four buildings still standing.

Called a "flamboyant piece of plumbing" and the symbol of "I Will," the tower today houses an art gallery, while the restored pumping station across the street is home to Lookingglass Theatre.

Hi, ho, come to the fair

1893 World's Columbian Exposition

In the late 1800s, world's fairs enabled cities and countries to show off their products, culture, and newest inventions. The US Congress selected Chicago to host what was supposed to be the 1892 World's Fair, marking the 400th anniversary of Christopher Columbus' arrival in the New World. The fair actually opened in 1893, but it was so successful that no one seemed to mind that it was late.

Chicagoans hoped the fair would show the world that the city was not a backwater western town but a bustling urban center with office skyscrapers; cultural institutions, including a new opera house; and a booming economy.

Called "the most famous world's fair ever held on American soil" by the *Chicago Tribune*, the World's Columbian Exposition indeed put Chicago on the map as a cosmopolitan city. Twenty-seven million

 ONLY IN CHICAGO

visits were tabulated, remarkable at a time when Chicago's population was just over one million.

Running 179 days, the fair was really two in one: the White City featured the exhibition buildings from various states and countries as well as those featuring horticulture, electricity, manufacturing and liberal arts, and art, while the Midway was for fun, where visitors enjoyed the exotic dancing of Little Egypt and the 264-foot Ferris wheel, the first of its kind.

The fair celebrated Chicago then, and its legacy lingers today.

Fact BOX

The 1893 World's Fair titillated tourists' tastes. Cream of Wheat, Aunt Jemima's pancake syrup, and Cracker Jack all made their debut, as did hamburgers, carbonated soda, and Wrigley's Juicy Fruit gum. A handheld snack, the brownie, came from the Palmer House Hotel, and Pabst Beer won its Blue Ribbon.

Chicago's Centennial Wheel: symbol of past and future

The Centennial Wheel anchors the amusement area of Chicago's Navy Pier, standing as a symbol of both the city's past and its future.

The first Ferris wheel inaugurated the 1893 World's Columbian Exposition, the world's fair that put Chicago on the map as a world-class city. The wheel, located on the fair's entertainment midway, was commissioned by officials hoping to secure for Chicago a structure that could "out-Eiffel" the Eiffel Tower, the symbolic structure built for the 1889 world's fair in Paris. The 264-foot wheel designed by George Ferris represented Chicago's move into the future; it wowed twenty-seven million fair visitors.

Fast forward to the 1990s, when Navy Pier was repurposed as a recreational facility. A Ferris wheel was added, tall enough to stand out from the low-lying pier buildings, visible from Lake Shore Drive, and lit up at night. It quickly became a major attraction.

In 2015, when the improvements that are evident today were begun on Navy Pier, a new wheel was commissioned. This one is 198 feet high—still not as tall as the 1893 wheel—consisting of forty-two gondolas outfitted with climate control for summer and winter conditions. At night, colored lights spin out from the hub along each spoke of the wheel. A special VIP gondola with a glass bottom allows for particularly spectacular views and photos.

Fact BOX

The Navy Pier Ferris wheel is twenty stories high, or 198 feet. What equals that height? According to Pier statistics: 396 Chicago-style hot dogs, 198 Chicago deep-dish pizzas, 23 Art Institute lion statues, 3.96 Picasso statues, and twice the total combined height of the 2017 Chicago Bulls basketball team.

ST. PATRICK'S DAY FIRE BOAT (page 28)

BUDDY GUY (page 158)

MUDDY WATERS (page 165)

16-INCH BASEBALL EQUIPMENT (page 69)

LAKE MICHIGAN (page 34)

4TH PRESBYTERIAN CHURCH (page 182)

WATER TOWER (page 80)

CULTURAL CENTER TIFFANY DOME (page 122)

CROWN FOUNTAIN AT MILLENNIUM PARK (page 116)

"L" TRAIN (page 76)

NORTH HALSTEAD STREET MARKER (page 45)

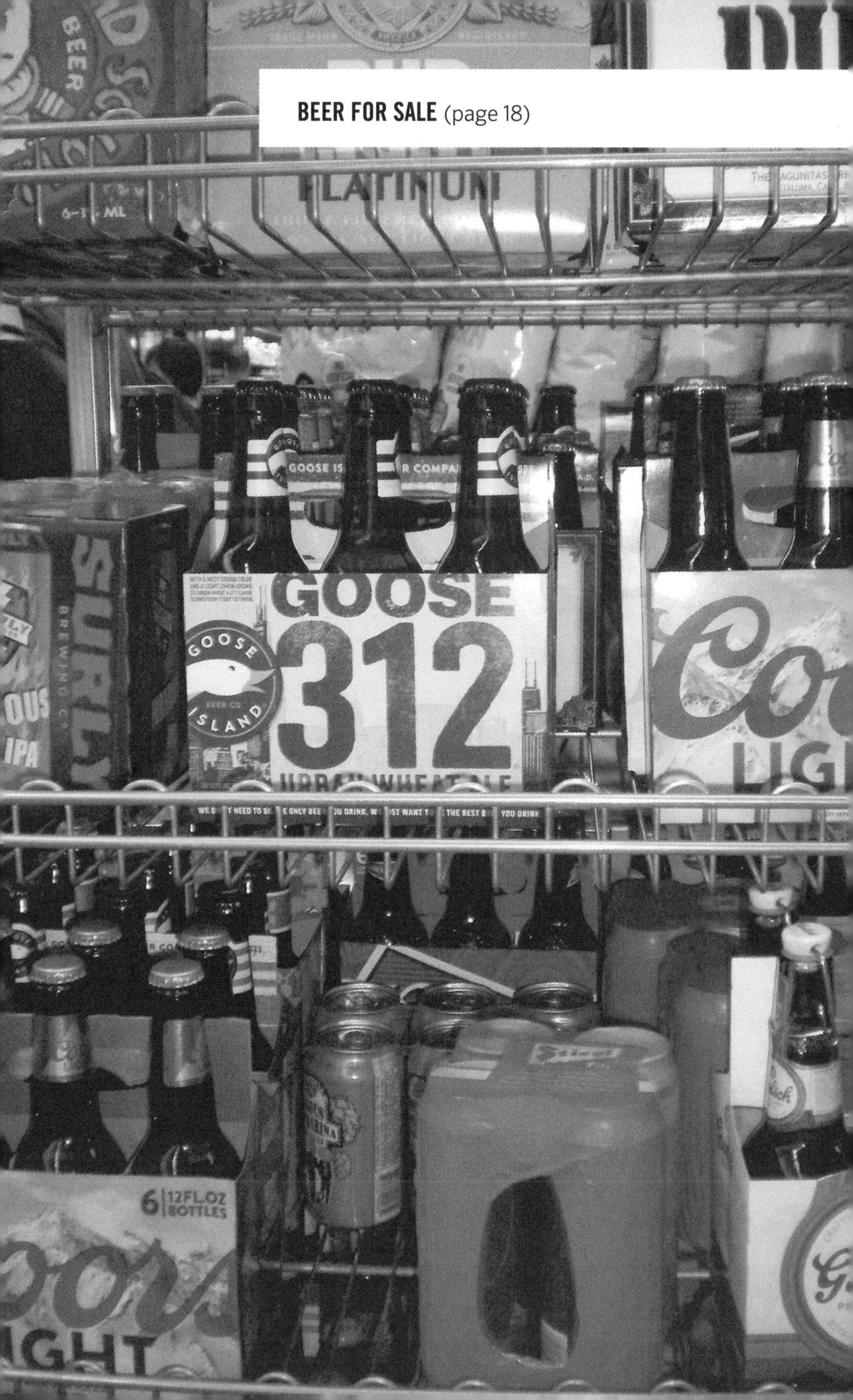

BEER FOR SALE (page 18)

America's first serial murderer

Henry H. Holmes, born Herman Webster Mudgett, grew up in New Hampshire. It's impossible to know how many people he murdered. He confessed to twenty-seven, but some estimates place the total closer to one hundred, and popular speculation boosts it to twice that. Holmes is identified by many as America's first serial killer.

Arriving in Chicago in 1885, at 63rd and Wallace streets, Holmes designed and built a hotel, nicknamed "The Castle" by local residents and later called the Murder Castle. The three-story building had more than sixty rooms, trapdoors, hidden staircases, secret passages, acid vats, and quicklime pits, where bodies could be disposed of. Also found were a blood-spattered dissecting table, torture devices, and even a crematorium, which was built into one of the walls.

Holmes used advertisements to find women who sought jobs or came for a marriage proposal. He wooed and seduced those coming to the city for the World's Columbian Exposition, which was called the White City, later killing them.

ONLY IN CHICAGO

Frank Geyer, a Philadelphia detective hunting Holmes for suspected earlier crimes, unraveled Holmes' past, in cooperation with his third wife, Georgiana, finally wise to her husband's ways.

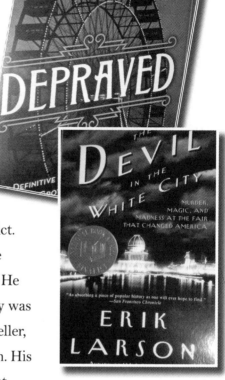

Holmes was tried in Philadelphia in 1895. The jury deliberated for less than three hours before returning a guilty verdict. He was hanged on May 7, 1896, nine days before his thirty-sixth birthday. He remained unrepentant. Holmes' story was popularized through the 2003 best-seller, *Devil in the White City*, by Eric Larson. His story still intrigues today: great-great-grandson Jeff Mudgett maintains that Holmes is also Jack the Ripper, the long anonymous English serial killer.

Fact BOX

A second World's Fair-era devil was Eugene Prendergast, a campaign volunteer who supported Mayor Carter Harrison's re-election, convinced that a Harrison victory would mean a city position for him. Harrison didn't know Prendergast. When no appointment was forthcoming, on October 28, 1893, Prendergast went to Harrison's home and shot him. Prendergast was convicted of the crime and hanged.

"Hot Time in the Old Town Tonight"

The Great Chicago Fire

October 1871 was a dry month. A drought had brought poor crops and many fires. On October 8, yet another fire broke out on the city's Near West Side and was fanned by strong winds. It overwhelmed the city's tired and undermanned fire department, lasting three days. By the time rain helped to finally extinguish the blaze, three hundred people had died, and hundreds of thousands of homes had been destroyed.

For decades, Mrs. Catherine O'Leary and her cow, Daisy, were blamed for starting the fire, as Daisy was said to have knocked over a lantern in the barn. In the words of the popular song, the cow "winked her eye and said, 'There'll be a hot time in the old town tonight.'" More recent scholarship also cites the lantern but postulates that it was likely Daniel "Peg Leg" Sullivan, a local drunk who was in the area at the time, who was responsible for knocking it over. Enough evidence was presented to convince the Chicago City Council in 1997 to exonerate the cow.

Although a devastating event for the city, the Great Fire burned out three-and-a-half square miles that became prime for redevelopment. The downtown business district was fair game for architects who came to Chicago eager to show their skills designing the new high-rise office buildings called "skyscrapers."

Fact Box

Jesuit Father Arnold Damen, founder of Holy Family Church, is credited with saving it in 1871 from the Great Chicago Fire. Legend says that Father Damen prayed to the Virgin Mary, promising that if the church were saved, he'd light candles. Winds shifted, and Holy Family was spared. Today, seven electric lights still shine on the altar.

The lake, the river, plus one fort, one fire, and two fairs

Chicago's flag

Chicago's flag is ubiquitous. Not only does it fly from municipal buildings, bridges, and flagpoles, but it's also found on police uniform patches, T-shirts, hats, keychains, beer labels, and tattoos. Anything that says "Chi-town" likely has a flag on it.

Its 100-year-old design of blue-and-white stripes with red stars celebrates the city's geography. The blue stripes represent the lake and the river and its branches. The white stripes remind us of the North, West, and South Side neighborhoods. Six-pointed stars speak of four notable historic events: Fort Dearborn, Chicago's original settlement; the Great Chicago Fire of 1871; and two World's Fairs, in 1893 and 1933.

 ONLY IN CHICAGO

The flag is a living, changing symbol. Designer Wallace Rice's 1917 original had only two stars. Many suggestions have been floated for a fifth or even sixth star—the Cubs' 2016 World Series win, anyone?—and rejected, but it still could happen.

A 2004 survey of vexillologists (those who study flags) ranked Chicago's as the nation's second-best municipal flag. Only Washington, DC's red-and-white stars and stripes topped it. Some think the popularity of today's Chicago flag was spurred by the 1990s influx of younger residents to downtown. As one writer noted, "In a divided Chicago, one thing we all agree on: a damn fine flag."

Stones on my tower

The base of Tribune Tower, a neo-Gothic landmark located north of the Chicago River on Michigan Avenue, is studded with more than 120 stones or fragments. Not just old rocks, these stones come from all over the world.

Each small piece, approximately six inches square, is labeled as to its origin. Pieces exist from the Great Wall of China and the Berlin Wall, from structures in all fifty states and countries around the globe. Colonel Robert R. McCormick, onetime owner and publisher of the *Chicago Tribune*, began collecting the pieces during World War, I before the tower was even built, with fragments from the city hall in Arras, France, and the cathedral at Ypres, in Belgium. According to writer Katherine Solomonson, McCormick was among many Americans who were "urged to hurry abroad" after the war so that they could take a piece of history home "before the battlefields were cleaned up."

ONLY IN CHICAGO

But McCormick didn't stop there. He subsequently assigned the *Tribune's* foreign correspondents to collect artifacts, gathering them as they gathered stories. "If you can get stones . . . from such buildings as the Law Court of Dublin, the Parthenon at Athens . . . or any other famous cathedral or place or ruins—possibly a piece of one of the pyramids—send them in," he wrote his reporters.

McCormick wanted correspondents to collect by "honorable means," although

some thought they were being given a license to steal. Whatever the means, the *Trib* called the contributions a "community endeavor" and a testament to the newspaper's international reach.

Fact BOX

The Gothic Revival design of Tribune Tower was the result of an international competition to create "the most beautiful office building in the world," held in 1922 by the *Chicago Tribune* newspaper. The winning entry by architecture firm Howells & Hood is based on the design of the cathedral at Rouen, France.

Rat-a-tat-tat

Al Capone and the Chicago Mob

When traveling and telling new acquaintances where they're from, Chicagoans report a common response: a fingers pointing to mimic a gun, accompanied by the staccato "Rat-a-tat-tat." Most Chicagoans would concede that the city's reputation for lawlessness began in the

1920s, courtesy of Al Capone.

A New Yorker, Capone arrived in 1919 to work for bootlegger Johnny Torrio. Speakeasies, the illicit social clubs that served liquor during Prohibition, flourished. Bootlegging was the city's chief vice. By 1920, the "outfit" had

a lock on that business. Making his headquarters in the Lexington Hotel on the Near South Side, Capone presided over the city's most infamous six years after he succeeded Torrio as head of the Chicago Syndicate in 1925.

In 1924, the city was home to approximately twenty thousand illegal retail liquor outlets. As Capone expanded his empire between

ONLY IN CHICAGO

1925 and 1932, there were 439 gangland slayings, most of them never solved. Capone, earning roughly $50 million annually, became a celebrity. Mayor William "Big Bill" Thompson, indebted to him for political and financial support, coddled the mob. Some considered Capone a folk hero.

Capone eliminated his rivals in a bloody gang war that culminated in the 1929 St. Valentine's Day Massacre, when hitmen killed seven rival mobsters, execution style, in a North Side garage. The slaughter capped the city's more than 300 gang-related murders during the decade.

FBI agent Eliot Ness and his team collected the evidence of income tax evasion that in 1931 put Capone behind bars. Capone's dynasty, however, would last well beyond his death in 1947.

Pop into Chicago's top tourist attraction

Garrett Popcorn Shops

Although city officials identify either Millennium Park or Navy Pier as Chicago's top tourist attraction, many Chicagoans might choose to differ. After all, where do you find long lines of people—lines that snake down the block and around corners? And whose shopping bag logo is seen most often on the arms of Loop or River North neighborhood pedestrians?

It's Garrett Popcorn Shops, a fixture on Chicago's retail scene since 1949.

The company credits its popularity to using "only the highest-quality ingredients" and the use of old-fashioned copper kettles. Garrett's "signature blend of kernels" is air popped in the shop and then mixed using "secret family recipes."

The most popular selection is Garrett Mix, a sweet-salty blend of CaramelCrisp and CheeseCorn. Another favorite purchase combines

ONLY IN CHICAGO

a trio of flavors: those two, plus salted or buttery popcorn, in a tin canister divided into three sections. The company also offers cashew, almond, pecan, and macadamia caramel popcorn as well as occasional seasonal flavors. All selections come in bags (rather than movie theater–style boxes), while the tins range in size from one gallon to six-and-a-half gallons.

Garrett's success has meant an expansion of the brand in Chicago, elsewhere in this country, and internationally. Shops can be found in Atlanta, Washington, DC, Las Vegas, New York, and other US cities. Abroad, they're scattered through much of the Far East, and there's also one in Dubai. Closer to home, the O'Hare International Airport shop is a favorite of tourists who want to take a bit of "Chicago" home.

Chicago's great urban playground

Millennium Park

To celebrate entering a new millennium, Mayor Richard M. Daley envisioned a wide swath of parkland replacing what existed in the 1990s along a stretch of Michigan Avenue south of the Chicago River: depressed railroad tracks and parking garages. Few thought the vision would be realized. It appeared the railroads owned the land, but the mayor's lawyers found ways, and Millennium Park debuted in 2004.

A twenty-first century space, Millennium Park was created using digital technology for design and construction. Promoting such activities as ice skating, water play, and concert going, it was constructed with sustainability in mind: utilizing electricity from solar panels, providing a green roof over the railroad tracks, and absorbing rainfall.

The twenty-five-acre northeast corner of Grant Park has become one of the city's top tourist attractions. It's also considered a template

 ONLY IN CHICAGO

for urban parks, which are no longer seen as places for passive recreation. In Millennium Park, visitors splash in Crown Fountain, where water cascades over fifty-foot glass-block towers with changing video images; gaze up at their image reflected in the mirrored surface of the Cloud Gate sculpture, better known as The Bean; and enjoy listening or dancing to nightly summer concerts ranging from classical to New Age.

A positive economic impact, or "Millennium Park effect," is what many cities seek. Since the park's opening, restaurants and hotels have popped up along Michigan Avenue near the park. More than ten thousand housing units were developed near the park in its first decade, and the area's pedestrian shopping traffic has increased substantially.

Reaching for the clouds

Chicago is home to the skyscraper. Originally called "cloud busters," these metal-frame buildings of ten stories or more are architecturally famous.

Two factors made Chicago ripe for tall buildings: the city's rapid industrial growth and the 1871 Great Chicago Fire. The blaze had eradicated downtown, leaving a *tabula rasa* of open land. Since the downtown was confined by the lake, the river, and railroad yards, buildings went vertical.

A plethora of what came to be known as Chicago-style commercial buildings went up between 1880 and 1920, all with similar construction: a metal frame with either brick or terra cotta cladding and tripartite design, with a base, a stack of floors, and a cornice atop. Many of the city's modern landmarks date to that era, including The Rookery, Marquette Building, and Railway Exchange Building.

A second round of skyscraper development came after World War II, this time in mid-century modernist style: sleek glass-and-steel construction with flat roofs and without applied ornamentation. These buildings dominated Chicago's streetscape from the 1950s through the 1990s. The most famous was also the tallest in the world when it was built in 1974: Sears Tower, now known as Willis Tower. It's lost its title as world's tallest but remains the tallest building in Chicago.

Today, contemporary high-rises and cranes dot the horizon as skyward building continues in Chicago.

CHICAGO'S TALLEST BUILDINGS

Fact BOX

The best way to see Chicago's skyscrapers is through the Chicago Architecture Foundation's eighty-five different tours, led by expert volunteer docents, on land, bus, or cruising the Chicago River.

Designing the new face of Chicago

In the wake of the 1871 Great Chicago Fire, architects flocked to Chicago to help rebuild the city. Many made names for themselves and became internationally famous.

Louis Sullivan, who arrived in 1873, advocated an "American architecture" based on natural design forms over older, neoclassical styles favored on the East Coast. With his partner, Dankmar Adler, Sullivan broke the mold with the 1889 Auditorium Building, which was built as a hotel and opera house and today is owned by Roosevelt University. Sullivan also gained fame for his architectural theories in *Kindergarten Chats* and other works and triumphed with the remarkable 1909 Schlesinger & Mayer department store, with its spectacular, curved wrought iron facade.

Sullivan's protégé, Frank Lloyd Wright, became America's most famous architect. Father of the twentieth century's Prairie Style

TALL, TALLER, TALLEST

LOUIS HENRI SULLIVAN

buildings, with horizontal lines that reflect the Midwest's flat prairie land, Wright designed numerous homes in and around Chicago. When he traveled to Germany, his *Wasmuth Portfolio* of drawings established his international reputation, which was buttressed with later work, including New York's Guggenheim Museum.

Ludwig Mies van der Rohe came to Chicago from Germany in 1938, eventually spreading his architectural vision with what today is called mid-century modernism: glass-and-steel high-rises with flat roofs and no applied ornamentation. It's a style that has been extremely popular worldwide since the 1950s.

Fact BOX

Today, contemporary architects, including Adrian Smith, designer of the world's tallest building, the Burj Khalifa, and Studio Gang's Jeanne Gang, create super-tall buildings around the world but still call Chicago home. It has been said correctly that "Chicago builds the world."

Tiffany treasures in Chicago

Look up and enjoy the view

Louis Comfort Tiffany may be identified with New York, where
he lived and worked, but Chicago features many Tiffany projects.
Besides the stained-glass windows found in many churches, Tiffany
& Co. was responsible for three major large-scale mosaic works in
Chicago.

The Chicago Cultural Center, a National Historic Landmark
built in 1897 as the city's library, features a neoclassical exterior
and sumptuous marble interior. The crowning highlight is Preston
Bradley Hall, with its thirty-eight-foot diameter Tiffany dome, said
to be the largest of its kind in the world. Incorporating colored
glass, stone, and mother of pearl, the dome dominates what was the
library's circulation area, space used today as a concert venue and
event facility.

A block away, the south atrium of the former Marshall Field's,
now Macy's, department store, is crowned by a Tiffany barrel vault

TALL, TALLER, TALLEST

ceiling, called the world's largest of its kind. Composed of tens of thousands of glass tesserae, the mosaic is done in the Art Nouveau style.

Elsewhere downtown, mosaic panels highlight the Marquette Building's two-story lobby, recounting in glass and mother of pearl the story of French Jesuit Father Jacques Marquette and his explorer partner Louis Joliet, who discovered and mapped the water route from the Great Lakes to the Gulf of Mexico. The panels were designed by Tiffany & Co.'s J.A. Holzer.

Monumental city

Chicago "boasts one of the world's great collections of public art," says *Chicago Tribune* architecture critic Blair Kamin. Public art is on display for all to appreciate, no matter its owner.

The collection originated in the nineteenth century, when public art meant statues of famous individuals, war heroes, politicians, or scientists. Chicago was dotted with such works, mostly in public parks.

Beginning in the late twentieth century, the city became home to skyscrapers with large plazas created to offset their height. Smart developers and city leaders sought to add art to the plazas, ushering in a golden age for public art. Some of the world's most renowned artists created art for Chicago locations: Pablo Picasso's *Untitled* at the Daley Center; Joan Miró's *The Sun, the Moon and One Star*, now known as "Miss Chicago," next to the Cook County Administration Building; Jean Dubuffet's *Monument with Standing Beast* in front of the State of Illinois' Thompson Center; and Alexander Calder's

TALL, TALLER, TALLEST

Flamingo in the Federal Center plaza. Marc Chagall's *Four Seasons* mosaic sits under its own roof in the plaza of the Chase Bank building.

Public art installations continue today not only in downtown but also throughout the city in newly constructed or renovated elevated train stations and neighborhood locations. A twenty-five-foot Abe Lincoln showed an almost-as-tall young man his Gettysburg Address, along Michigan Avenue; a twenty-foot doe walked along the Riverwalk, and painted and decorated trees dotted local parks in 2017, the Year of Public Art, when many works were highlighted.

Fact BOX

The 1967 Installation of Pablo Picasso's *Untitled* created a storm of criticism. "What is it?" was the cry. Speculation that it represented an Afghan hound or perhaps a woman didn't sit well, but over the years, "The Picasso," as it's called, has been embraced by Chicagoans, particularly the children. In 2017, a fiftieth birthday party celebrated the sculpture.

An American home for the middle class

The British first used the word "bungalow" to describe the one-story houses with large, encircling porches they encountered in Bengal, India. In the late 1890s, the bungalow style was exported to California, where it meant a one-story house with a wide porch. Bungalows were simple and well built, fit in with their environment, were created of local materials, and were modestly priced. Sears, Roebuck & Co. helped spread the bungalow's popularity by offering many designs in its mail-order catalog.

Chicago, with a climate that in no way resembled that of either India or California, created its own version of the bungalow: brick, no encircling porch, one-and-a-half stories, with a low-pitched hipped roof and wide overhangs. Many of the houses featured leaded art-glass windows. More than eighty thousand bungalows were built between 1919 and 1930, spread in an arc, called the "Bungalow Belt,"

TALL, TALLER, TALLEST

of four to seven miles from downtown. Chicago bungalows embodied the American dream.

Bungalows lost their luster in the latter half of the twentieth century, but now, as many of the dwellings turn one hundred, there has been a resurgence of interest. The Chicago Bungalow Initiative, launched by the City of Chicago in 2001, helps promote awareness and appreciation of this building type and advises homeowners on various issues, such as ways to rehab and update homes, and energy efficiency.

What's that you say?

Chicago's street names come from a variety of sources, but Chicagoans may not pronounce a particular name the way the person who christened the street did.

Take the street named for Wolfgang Amadeus Mozart, one of the greats of classical music. Chicagoans don't use the German pronunciation *MOTZ-art*; they say *MO-zart*, with an emphasis on the "z."

Johann Wolfgang von Goethe, perhaps the greatest of all German poets, also has his name mangled. The street named for him, on the North Side in an area that was settled by German immigrants in the 1850s and '60s, isn't pronounced in the German way, *GER-ta*. The Chicago version is *GO-thee*, so totally non-German that it's remarkable the descendants of German immigrants haven't complained. Perhaps it's simply that other immigrants can't pronounce the German.

ON THE STREETS WHERE WE LIVE

Then there's Devon Avenue, today the commercial center of an Asian Indian settlement that's lined with sari shops and restaurants. It was named by the developer of the Edgewater neighborhood, John L. Cochran, for his hometown on the Main Line commuter rail service running west from Philadelphia. Devon, Pennsylvania, was likely named for Devonshire, the English county, but despite the name's origins, in Chicago, Devon is pronounced *De-VON*, not the British *DEV-on.*

Fact BOX

Since 1984, some streets display two street signs. Installed below the original green signs are additional brown ones that are commemorative. The word "Honorary" is flanked by four stars. These signs recognize individuals who've made contributions to the city. Nominations come from an alderman's office and require city council approval before installation.

The under-pinnings of Chicago's map

Chicago's street grid

Chicago was laid out in the 1830s by surveyor James Thompson. He drew the streets on a grid, with straight lines and right angles, and began the practice of naming streets for famous, wealthy, and powerful people.

Through to the 1890s, when Chicago grew at a prodigious rate, the city annexed additional land, which sometimes included streets with the same names as existing ones. According to *Streetwise: Chicago*, by 1893, Chicago had "17 Lincoln streets, avenues, or places; while some streets had six or seven different names in different places."

The city's uniform street numbering system was originated by Edward P. Brennan, a nonplanner who chaired the City Club of Chicago's Committee on Street Names in 1908. He designated

ON THE STREETS WHERE WE LIVE

State and Madison streets as the base for numbering, with each 800 in an address—denoting eight blocks—indicating a mile, and the distance from the baseline. This is still today's system, although on the oldest streets, numbering is slightly less precise. Brennan also decreed even numbers on the north side of a street and odd numbers on the south for east-west streets, and even numbers on the west and odd on the east for north-south streets.

Finally, it was also Brennan who, in 1913, began using one name for all portions of a street even if it had separated segments and didn't run in a continuous line.

Fact BOX

Southern Illinois mapmaker James Thompson named one of the city's major east-west thoroughfares for his home county, Randolph. As payment for his work, Thompson was offered downtown Chicago land, but he chose not to accept. Instead, he took home a horse.

Street-wise

As of the 1990s, the Chicago metropolitan area boasted 54,600 miles of streets and roads, including 2,500 miles of expressways, 17,300 miles of highways and arterial streets, and 34,800 miles of local streets. In about half of the city, streets are numbered; elsewhere, they carry noun designations: names of people, places, trees, or destinations.

Many record the city's history with the names of early settlers. For example, there's (Mark) Beaubien Court, named for the innkeeper and fur trader who opened the Sauganash Hotel in 1833, and Jean Avenue, named after Jean Baptiste Point DuSable, the city's first settler.

Some roads tell you where you are: Indian Road in the northern part of the city runs along what was a Native-American settlement, while Western Avenue was at one point the city's western boundary.

Then there are streets that honor famous people: Sheridan Road, for General Philip Sheridan of Civil War fame; Martin Luther King Jr. Drive, for the civil rights leader; early US presidents Washington, Adams, Jefferson, Madison, and Monroe, although the streets aren't necessarily arrayed in presidential order.

ON THE STREETS WHERE WE LIVE

Other observers believe the city's street names reflect Chicago's personality. Authors of the March 2017 *Chicago* magazine article "67 Reasons to Love Chicago" note, as Reason 7: ". . . [O]ur Street Names are Tough: Wacker, Cermak, Pulaski, Hoyne, Gunnison, Lunt. They sound like fists hitting meat."

Fact BOX

One road with myriad names, The Drive, Outer Drive, LSD, or, officially, since 1946, Lake Shore Drive, runs more than sixteen miles alongside Lake Michigan. In the late 1920s, the section from the Chicago River to 57th Street was dubbed Leif Erikson Drive, for the Viking explorer.

Proudly identifying with the local parish

Chicago's North and South sides are different. East-west streets on the South Side are numbered; up north, there is one street name after another, making it difficult at times to determine where you're headed. Also, depending on whether they live north or south of Madison Street, where all street numbering begins, Chicagoans identify where they live differently.

On the North Side, "Where are you from?" or "Where did you grow up?" is usually answered with a neighborhood name: "I'm from Rogers Park" . . . or Lakeview, Sauganash, or any other North Side neighborhood. The reply is easily understood. The same could be true for South Siders, if they responded to the query with "South Shore," "Hyde Park," or "Hegewisch."

ON THE STREETS
WHERE WE LIVE

But many native South and Southwest Siders don't reply that way. They tend to identify where they grew up or where they live by the name of the local Roman Catholic parish.

Originally, neighborhood Catholic churches were established to serve specific ethnic groups. The Archdiocese of Chicago approved of separate churches for Irish, Italians, and Germans through the 1920s. Close ties between churches and immigrant populations, with churches providing services for the newly arrived, continues today, generating ongoing identification with the local houses of worship.

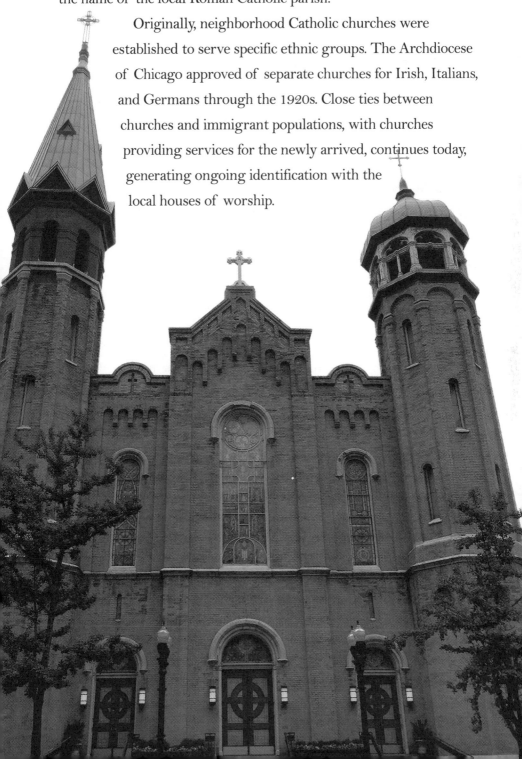

Get your kicks on Route 66

Driving the Mother Road

"There is no greater highway in the history of America than Route 66—the Mother Road," says author Troy Taylor in *Weird Illinois*.

Route 66, which stretches 2,500 miles to Santa Monica, California, begins in Chicago. America's first cross-country route harks back to the days of families traversing the country along two-lane highways, stopping at local diners for homemade food and overnight at small motor courts, precursors to post–World War II motels. The road, which was opened in 1926 as part of the country's first federal road system, has been called America's most famous highway, even though officially it no longer exists intact.

Some 80 percent of Route 66 to California is still drivable, though less in Illinois than in other states. Many of those who chase their dreams on Route 66 are bikers riding huge motorcycles and traveling in groups across the country or history buffs who enjoy the individually owned-and-operated kitschy architecture in restaurants

**ON THE STREETS
WHERE WE LIVE**

and gas stations that still exist along the route.

The *Chicago Tribune* has called Route 66 "a museum, a trove of quirky culture venerated in song, cinema, and literature." Singer Nat King Cole's "(Get Your Kicks on) Route 66" still reverberates among those seeking to follow its route, and efforts are currently under way to designate Route 66 a National Historic Trail.

Fact BOX

The cross-country Route 66 began and ended in the heart of downtown Chicago. Today, signs on Adams Street at Michigan Avenue and on Jackson Boulevard mark its beginning and end, although these streets weren't one-way when the road was built.

Underground Chicago: the Pedway

Keeping yourself dry in drippy weather

Chicago's unique "city under a city" is the pedestrian walkway dubbed the Pedway, a network threaded among more than forty downtown city blocks south of the Chicago River, connected through tunnels, ground-level concourses, and overhead bridges. More than fifty buildings are linked by five miles of mostly underground walkways, and tens of thousands of Chicagoans use the path every weekday. (Some sections are closed on weekends.)

Begun in the 1950s with one-block tunnel connections between Chicago's two subway lines, today the Red and Blue line stations at Washington and Jackson streets, the Pedway travels west under major government buildings and east to the Lake Shore East residential development. A northern section passes under Illinois Center, primarily an office complex, while shorter sections connect individual buildings or traverse parking garages.

ON THE STREETS
WHERE WE LIVE

From the 1970s, the city has had three goals for Pedway expansion: link pedestrian traffic generators with transportation facilities, provide weather-protected walkways throughout downtown, and enable pedestrians to avoid the air and noise pollution of vehicular traffic.

Today, the Pedway is perceived in two different ways. Some people avoid it because they consider it difficult to navigate and fear getting lost, but many consider it a boon, particularly downtown condo and apartment residents, who can travel throughout the Loop and by public transportation as far as O'Hare International Airport without ever getting their feet wet.

Different directions and levels: It's Wacker Drive

Chicago's amazing many-faceted street

Wacker Drive runs two ways: Beginning as an east-west street paralleling the south side of the Chicago River, it becomes a north-south thoroughfare as it follows the east side of the river's South Branch. Wacker Drive is also multilevel, with three levels in some areas and two in others. The configuration results from city planning in the late nineteenth and early twentieth centuries.

Beer baron Charles Wacker, chair of the Chicago Plan Commission from 1909 to 1926, was one of myriad civic leaders who argued for preservation of the lakefront and against downtown traffic congestion. Accordingly, he suggested relocating South Water

**ON THE STREETS
WHERE WE LIVE**

Street Market (primarily a produce market) out of downtown and rebuilding South Water Street into a double-decked road. When completed, the street was renamed Wacker for him, and another road took the name of South Water.

Wacker had served as a director of the 1893 World's Columbian Exposition, where architect Daniel Burnham was director of operations. Wacker supported Burnham's efforts in city planning. To promote Burnham's *1909 Plan of Chicago*, Wacker provided copies of a textbook about it, called *Wacker's Manual*, to Chicago's middle-school students.

Wacker Drive, with its neoclassical design, is also the backdrop to Chicago's Riverwalk. When the road was refurbished in the 1990s, openings were created from the street to allow for restaurant storage space along the new Riverwalk.

Fact BOX

Lower Wacker Drive, one of the street's three levels, offers motorists the fastest way to cross the Loop, away from street-level traffic. The swift route is helped by the fact many people either don't know about it or don't know how to navigate it.

It's cooler by the lake

Chicago's volatile weather

Chicagoans joke that if you don't like the weather, wait an hour. In that time, on a sunny, seventy-degree day, the temperature can dive fifteen degrees, sending everyone scurrying for jackets. The culprit is the wind blowing in off Lake Michigan, but it has different effects in different seasons.

In the summer, wind coming off the lake keeps lakefront temperatures several degrees lower than temperatures inland—the "cooler by the lake" relief that caused the pre-air-conditioned homes of the wealthy to be built on Lake Michigan's shores. In the winter, though, the lake creates a warming effect, since the water is warmer than the air, meaning that temperatures downtown are slightly higher than in the rest of the city and inland suburbs.

For Chicago's neighbors, "lake effect" means more snow in parts of Indiana and Michigan than in Illinois. In a typical winter, the eastern shore of the lake gets 60 to 100 percent more snow than the western, or Illinois, side.

Chicago is a city of four seasons: Winter here is cold with snow, summer is hot with high humidity, and fall's glorious days of

 WEATHER

mild temperatures and sunshine never last long enough. Spring is extremely unpredictable, with dramatic temperature fluctuations, lingering snow in some years, and often lots of rain.

Please Keep Floor Dry... **Wet** Bag

RECORD HIGH: 100° (1947)   RECORD LOW: 33° (19

ves on gusty wind

| 70s | 80s | 90s | 100s | 110s |

An unseasonably low pressure center across the upper Mid on Thursday, spawnin thunderstorms across region. The storms eru in somewhat humid air ahead of a cold front, w temperatures rose to the low and mid-80s. Behin the front, winds gusting over 35 mph swept au-tumnlike air in from the northwest. Late afternoon temperatures were held in the 50s and low 60s across much of Minnesota and northern Iowa. This air wi flow across the Chicago

Concord 85/64
Buffalo 86/62 Albany 86/70
etroit 4/58 Cleveland 81/62 Boston 82/68
New York 83/73
Pittsburgh 85/59
Washington 90/71
t. Louis 80/61 Louisville 79/59 Charlotte 85/70

Fact BOX

Chicago's temperatures range from January's average 6.9 days of zero degrees or below to July's 7.8 days of ninety degrees or above. The average wind speed in the city is 10.3 miles per hour, with gusts ranging from forty-eight to sixty-nine miles per hour. Precipitation averages more than thirty-three inches per year.

Windy City revisited

Does the volatile Chicago weather give rise to the city's temperament? Maybe.

The Windy City, Chicago's oft-used nickname, doesn't refer to the city's wind. While the city is often buffeted by gusting winds off Lake Michigan, the name referred to the excessive bragging done by local politicians who were lobbying for the 1892 World's Columbian Exposition to be held in Chicago rather than in New York, Washington, DC, or St. Louis. Chicago landed the fair, although it held the event a year late.

Today, many Chicagoans exhibit a similar aggressive boastfulness, now to counter negative comments about the city. As local public television reporter and producer Geoffrey Baer has noted, "Chicago boosterism is in our DNA."

President Donald Trump didn't gain many friends in Chicago when he repeatedly criticized the city for its high rate of violent crime and threatened to send troops to stem the violence. Not that Chicagoans don't abhor the situation and haven't been trying to turn it around, but as *Chicago* magazine's writers put it when they came

 WEATHER

out swinging with a "Why We Love Chicago" issue in March 2017, they had to "punch back" because "we're tired of our city getting knocked around."

Chicago takes its Windy City title seriously.

Fact BOX

The windiest city in the United States is not the one nicknamed the Windy City. Among large cities, Chicago ranks twelfth for average wind speed. America's windiest major city is Boston, where the wind blows, on average, two miles per hour faster than in Chicago.

The snow that blew in a mayor

Blizzard upends city

Between January 12 and 14, 1979, a total of 20.7 inches of snow fell on Chicago, on top of the eight inches that had blanketed the city two weeks earlier. Though Democratic Mayor Michael Bilandic appeared on TV news shows to reassure residents that streets were being plowed and schoolyards made available for parking, city crews simply could not keep up. The schoolyards remained covered in snow, ice, and slush, and residents fumed.

The city's failure to cope with the blizzard became the key issue in the mayoral primary held the following month. Jane Byrne, a Democrat and commissioner of consumer affairs under the late Mayor Richard J. Daley, had been fired by Bilandic, and many observers believed that her mayoral candidacy was

WEATHER

motivated by a desire for retribution. But the way the city had dealt with the snow emergency overrode that concern. Garbage had not been collected, mass transit had been unable to keep up with the increased number of riders, and it was revealed that the city's "snow emergency plan" was less than satisfactory.

The result: Byrne defeated Bilandic, the choice of the Democratic machine, in the primary. She then easily beat the Republican in the general election, going on to serve one four-year term and becoming Chicago's only woman mayor.

Fact BOX

With a heavy Chicago snowfall, residents find shovels and chairs. Although side streets will eventually be plowed by the city, they are usually cleared first by local residents. Shovel-wielding citizens then place their chairs or trash cans, milk cartons, whatever they can find in the spot to reserve it. They have "dibs" on it.

Top-notch, award-winning

Chicago regional theaters shine

New York may be America's center for theater, but Chicago is right up there, with Tony Award-winning regional theaters, innumerable small venues, and large downtown theaters that host Broadway touring shows.

As of 2017, five Chicago theaters had won the Regional Theatre Tony Award, reflecting the city's theatrical depth.

Steppenwolf Theatre, winner in 1985, is an ensemble company begun in the mid-1970s by several high school friends who wanted to put on plays. They launched their theater in a church basement in north suburban Highland Park. Its home now is on the city's North Side. Steppenwolf has been described by critics as providing a "muscular, no-holds-barred, fearless brand of acting that screams 'Chicago'."

The Goodman Theatre, the 1992 winner, is the oldest of the Tony honorees, dating to the 1920s. Its subscription season features

THE PLAY'S THE THING

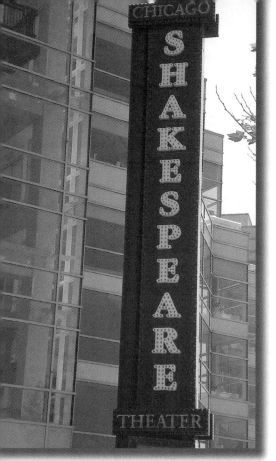

diverse productions, including occasional musicals and the annual *A Christmas Carol.*

The 2001 winner, Victory Gardens Theater, has its home in the refurbished Biograph Theater, originally a movie house, where it presents new works by new playwrights that often tackle contemporary issues.

Chicago Shakespeare Theater, the 2008 Tony winner, has three stages to accommodate audiences ranging from 150 to 850. The Shakespearean-style Courtyard Theater, a thrust stage, hosts most of the Bard's productions, while the smaller, flexible-seating Upstairs theater and the new Yard theater, with its movable towers of seats, allow the company to offer myriad productions from all over the world.

Finally, Lookingglass Theatre Company, 2011 winner, performs in the city's old water-pumping station, presenting dramas that in many cases incorporate circus-style action.

In city storefronts, out in the suburbs

Area's thriving theater scene

It's in storefronts and small theaters and on stages tucked away in church basements and school buildings that the heart of Chicago theater beats. Large downtown houses and major regional theaters may draw the limelight, but the legions of promising new actors, beginning song-and-dance folk, and familiar character actors keep off-Loop theaters jumping as well.

Theaters in Chicago trace their ancestry to James McVicker, who brought first-class dramas to the city in the Civil War era. He built a theater on Madison Avenue between Dearborn and State

 THE PLAY'S THE THING

streets, where he barred prostitutes, rowdies, and alcohol. Renowned actor Edwin Booth (who married McVicker's daughter, Mary) trod the boards there, as did brother John Wilkes.

Theatrical productions are by no means limited to city venues. Chicago boasts a robust suburban theater scene, with musicals, dramas, and comedies staged both indoors and out. Exciting theater can be experienced in subscription seasons to the north, at Skokie's Northlight Theatre and Glencoe's Writers Theater, the northwest suburban Marriott Theatre in Lincolnshire, and to the west at Drury Lane Theatre in Oakbrook Terrace, the latter two specializing in musical theater productions.

Still in the city but far south of downtown in the Hyde Park neighborhood, Court Theatre presents classic drama on the University of Chicago campus.

Second City? Second to none!

It's a comedy club—its name a winking reference to *New Yorker* writer A.J. Liebling's snide label for Chicago—but it's a lot more: Ever since Second City opened its doors in December 1959, it has been hailed as a center of satire, cabaret of contemporary humor, and starter home for a who's who of comedy greats.

The club was opened in a former Chinese laundry on North Wells Street in the city's Old Town neighborhood by three University of Chicago grads exploring improvisational theater concepts. Almost immediately, Second City set a standard for smart social and political satire.

The troupe, whose early members included Mike Nichols, Joan Rivers, and Del Close, became known early on for brainy wit with spoofs of academia, such as "Football Comes to the University of Chicago," a sketch that had a coach who couldn't teach students

 THE PLAY'S THE THING

football because they referred to the football as a "demi-poly-tetrahedron."

In 1967, Second City moved down the street into a bigger venue. The 1960s and '70s brought more changes and a new generation of comic icons, including John Belushi and Harold Ramis, who created a style of comedy reflecting the radical attitudes of the time.

In 1975, when Lorne Michaels and others launched TV music-and-sketch comedy show *Saturday Night Live*, the cast was stocked with Second City alums, including Dan Aykroyd and Gilda Radner. That only perpetuated Second City's reputation as a breeding ground for up-and-coming comic talents, such as Bill Murray, Stephen Colbert, and Tina Fey. The troupe has continued to provide players to the show.

Early Hollywood

Filming begins at Essanay Studios

Despite the association of Hollywood, California, with movie making, America's film industry actually began in Chicago.

At the 1893 World's Fair, Thomas Edison displayed his kinetoscope, a cabinet-like device with a film loop that passed in front of the viewer peering through a peephole. That inspired George K. Spoor, a native of north suburban Highland Park. The following year he discovered how to direct light through a lens to illuminate images on a wall. At about the same time, Chicago-born inventor William N. Selig created a camera and projector and began making and distributing commercial films.

In 1907, Spoor formed a partnership with Gilbert Anderson, one of the leading actors in Edison's company. After a year, their Peerless Film Manufacturing Co. was transformed into Essanay Studios, which became home to silent film stars, such as Charlie Chaplin, Francis X. Bushman, Wallace Beery, and Gloria Swanson. Other production companies also flourished, among them Ebony

 THE PLAY'S THE THING

FAMOUS PLAYERS-LASKY CORPORATION

Film Corporation, probably the United States' first African American owned-and-operated film studio.

Chicago was a logical location for filming in the early twentieth century: Investment capital was available, the city's industrial base supported the production companies, and access to railroads meant that studios could transport their films almost anywhere in the US within three days.

Almost as quickly as the film industry developed, however, it left Chicago. The problem was the weather: not enough sunny days, winter days that were too short and cold for shooting outdoors, and audiences' preference for outdoor scenes. The movies went west to Hollywood.

Fact BOX

Although movies may have left Chicago, one reminder of movie history remains: the stone arch from the building of Famous Players Lasky Corporation, parent company of Paramount Pictures. The façade is fittingly housed in the Jeanne Gang-designed Media Production Center building, home to Columbia College Chicago's film department.

"Joyous hand-clapping, foot-tapping, aisle-dancing" music

Chicago: birthplace of gospel

"Gospel, an American style of religious music, traces its roots to American folk music, African American spirituals, and early blues and jazz," explains John Russick in *Encyclopedia of Chicago*. Gospel was born in the African American churches of Chicago's South Side.

Thomas A. Dorsey, often called the father of gospel music, was key to gospel's spread. He composed many of the most celebrated songs, including "Take My Hand, Precious Lord," and coined the phrase "gospel songs," giving the musical genre a name.

Dorsey began his Chicago career at Ebenezer Baptist Church where, in 1931, he and Theodore Frye organized the first modern gospel chorus. In 1933, he, Frye, and Magnolia Lewis Butts

MUSIC AND ART

established the national Convention of Gospel Choirs and Choruses, which extended the music's reach.

It was Dorsey's lengthy service as choir director at Pilgrim Baptist Church that perpetuated the popularity of the music and its artists, who included Sallie and Roberta Martin and Mahalia Jackson. Recordings of gospel music issued in the mid-1920s, and nationally aired radio church services

beginning in 1935 propelled the new genre, a combination of church hymns with African American tonality and rhythms.

Chicago was "gospel central" when Jackson, fellow gospel queen Albertina Walker, Soul Stirrers members Sam Cooke and Johnny Taylor, and the Staple Singers all called the city home. Gospel continues to have a Chicago presence, but in the 1970s, the center of gospel moved to California.

Chicago sings the blues

African American music refined in the city

African Americans who migrated to Chicago from the Mississippi Delta brought with them twelve-bar country blues music. Crossing that with Northern electric guitar sounds gave birth to the Chicago-style blues. Chicago was fertile ground for the new urban sound, as its hundreds of thousands of African American residents provided a ready market.

The original bluesmen came in the 1910s. Such artists as "Big Bill" Broonzy popularized

 MUSIC AND ART

a guitar style based on urban themes. In the 1940s, musicians added amplification, and by the 1950s, Chicago was the capital of hard-driving electric blues exemplified by "Muddy Waters," Chicago's most famous bluesman. Born McKinley Morganfield, Waters became king of Chicago blues with such classics as "Hoochie Coochie Man" and "Rollin' and Tumblin.'" He won six Grammy Awards before he died in 1983 at age 86.

The blues tradition was nurtured at Chicago's famous Maxwell Street Market, now gone, but during its heyday, the place to shop for everything from suits to nuts. Blues musicians made their names playing outdoors before recording for Chicago record labels.

The golden age of Chicago blues, according to Maxwell Street historian Tom Smith, influenced more than just Americans. British groups, such as the Yardbirds, Led Zeppelin, and The Rolling Stones, all incorporated blues into their music. The Rolling Stones even took their name from a Muddy Waters song.

Fact BOX

Buddy Guy's Legends is one of the city's most popular blues clubs. Guy, a Rock and Roll Hall of Fame inductee and Grammy Award winner, pioneered electric blues, playing with Howlin' Wolf and Muddy Waters after he arrived in Chicago in 1957. He still plays and hopes the club will help keep the blues alive.

And all that jazz

New Orleans comes to Chicago

Jazz, a hybrid of West African rhythms, banjo music, and barrelhouse piano, originated in New Orleans at the turn of the twentieth century. Following the First World War, however, when African Americans began moving north in large numbers during the Great Migration, Chicago became the Midwest center for jazz. Among New Orleans jazz men who moved north with their bands was Louis "Satchmo" Armstrong, who came to Chicago in 1922, joining another New Orleans expat, Joseph "King" Oliver and his Creole Jazz Band.

Jazz musicians played primarily in Chicago's African American neighborhood on the Near South Side that was originally dubbed the Black Belt and later Bronzeville. Numerous clubs booked African American jazz groups that "pulsated with the sounds of Dixieland and with Armstrong's 'Gut Bucket Blues,'" producing

MUSIC AND ART

a unique Chicago sound that fused jazz and blues together, according to *Ethnic Chicago* author Richard Lindberg.

Other musicians had migrated earlier from the South: pianists Tony Jackson and Ferdinand La Menthe "Jelly Roll" Morton. They made the city a hothouse for new music, but it was Armstrong, argues *Chicago Tribune* jazz critic Howard Reich, who "lit the fuse" and transformed what was somewhat crude Southern-style jazz into a bona fide art form with its significant features: scat singing and an emphasis on individual solos.

Chance the Rapper

Chicago's top rap entertainer, booster

Called "hip-hop's big dreamer," a young rapper looms large on Chicago's music and philanthropic scenes. Born Chancellor Johnathan Bennett in 1993, the man known professionally as Chance the Rapper is a music producer, activist, and philanthropist from the South Side Chatham neighborhood.

Chance's music is the basis of his fame. In 2013, his third mixtape, "Coloring Book," earned three Grammy awards, including Best Rap Album. It was the first streaming-only album to be nominated for a Grammy, and the first to win one. According to Common, a fellow Grammy-winning recording artist, Chance "upends expectations about what artists, especially hip-hop artists, can do." Streaming his albums rather than selling them gives him independence, without the support of a record label. The music, much of which reflects Chance's Christian perspective, isn't geared to one age group, race, or gender, but covers them all.

 MUSIC AND ART

In November 2014, Chance was named Chicago's Outstanding Youth of the Year by Chicago Mayor Rahm Emanuel. He actively fights gun violence, both in his hometown and nationally, through numerous campaigns. In March 2017, Chance announced a donation of $1 million to the Chicago Public Schools to help offset the lack of state funding. It was, he said, "a call to action" against politics as usual. As Common says, "He gives back to his community." *Chicago Tribune* writer Dahleen Glanton also highlighted Chance's offstage impact in a July 2017 column: "Chance also is an activist for justice, a voice of reason, and a vivid reminder that young black men are worth fighting for."

Rock 'n' roll, rhythm and blues

Chess Records created music history

Leonard and Phil Chess, co-owners of Chess Records, were music pioneers. At a time when most companies wouldn't record African American artists, Chess did, placing it at the forefront of blues, rhythm and blues, and a new genre, rock 'n' roll.

The Polish-born Chess brothers immigrated to Chicago and ran South Side jazz clubs. In the late 1940s, Leonard took control of Aristocrat Records, renaming it Chess Records in 1950. The first Chess release was saxophonist Gene Ammons' "My Foolish Heart," a hit. It was followed by Muddy Waters' "Rollin' Stone."

Through the 1950s, Chess signed a slew of blues, rhythm and blues, and rock 'n' roll artists, including Bo Diddley, Sonny Boy Williamson, and Chuck Berry. While Phil focused on jazz, Leonard homed in on "roots" music, making Chess the greatest repository of blues. In July 1955, Chess released Chuck Berry's "Maybellene," which promptly hit the pop charts. Chess' roster in the 1960s

 MUSIC AND ART

expanded to include Etta James and Koko Taylor. Leonard also became involved in Chicago radio as part owner of WVON-AM, a black-oriented radio station.

The legendary label promoted rock 'n' roll with teenagers like Ike Turner, who recorded "Rocket 88." When Elvis Presley hit big, Chess got its own white rock 'n' rollers, Dale Hawkins and Bobby Charles. Many of the label's biggest hits came from doo-wop groups, such as the Moonglows.

Fact BOX

Today, the Willie Dixon Blues Heaven Foundation is located on the site of Chess Records' 1960s home. Although the Chess brothers ran the company, many maintain that Willie Dixon, an African American ex-boxer, musician, songwriter, and producer, ran the sessions for almost every blues recording.

The sweetest sounds

Classical music and opera

Classical music and opera arose with Chicago's late nineteenth century development, when city fathers recognized that any city deemed world-class needed a home for European opera. Entrepreneur Ferdinand Peck persuaded fellow businessmen to invest in an opera house in time for the 1893 World's Columbian Exposition. Designed by prominent architects Adler & Sullivan, today's Auditorium Theatre is a visual and aural delight.

Originally home to what is now the Chicago Symphony Orchestra as well as opera, the theater's 1889 Auditorium Building sparkles with Louis Sullivan

MUSIC AND ART

designs and unmatched acoustics and sight lines created by Dankmar Adler. Used today for music and dance performances, the Auditorium, now owned by Roosevelt University, continues to host culture.

Opera moved from the Auditorium in the late 1920s after Chicago businessman Samuel Insull opened his own location—today's Civic Opera House, home to Chicago's Lyric Opera. Lyric, among the nation's leading opera companies, presents an annual series of opera and musical theater.

The Chicago Symphony Orchestra (CSO) also departed the Auditorium, seeking a site for subscription concerts. The result was the 1904 Orchestra Hall, now known as Symphony Center, designed by starchitect Daniel Burnham, a CSO trustee. The orchestra's first music director, Theodore Thomas, whose name is incised on the building, set the orchestra on its path to classical music eminence in the world today, under world-renowned Music Director Riccardo Muti.

A town that loves to party

Chicago is a summer festival

On any summer weekend, you'll find Chicagoans heading to a festival. Beginning in late May, festivals pop up everywhere, and they continue through the end of September.

The city is a big promotor of fests, with fests dedicated to gospel, blues, and jazz, as well as classical music offered in Millennium Park, and the massive five-day Taste of Chicago food fest, also accompanied by musical acts, in Grant Park. Large commercially organized music celebrations, such as Lollapalooza and the Pitchfork Festival, provide several music stages for different acts over long weekends. Food vendors gather for outdoor tastings in various neighborhoods, though sometimes, as with Ribfest, one food is featured, with chefs presenting their favorite preparations.

Art fairs show off fine art and crafts in neighborhoods as diverse as the

MUSIC AND ART

Gold Coast, Hyde Park, and Old Town. June's Printers Row Lit
Fest promises two days of book selling and author talks. Chicago's
Fiestas Puertorriqueñas and Puerto Rican People's Parade, a four-
day annual Latino cultural event, is one of the largest in the United
States. In August, the city hosts the Chicago Air and Water Show,
and Bronzeville's huge back-to-school Bud Billiken parade marks the
end of summer.

That Chicagoans appreciate and participate in the festivals is
evident in that most are sold out, and huge crowds gather at the
free city-sponsored affairs.

The Art Institute of Chicago

and other museums

Chicago's love affair with learning

Name a topic and you'll likely find a museum in Chicago that covers it, whether it's art, science, literature, poetry, botany, or zoology. The cultural bounty doesn't end there, because museums of Chicago history, ethnic history, Middle Eastern archeology, surgical medicine, and broadcast communications are also available.

Chicago's museum-going began in 1856 with the founding of the Chicago Historical Society, today the Chicago History Museum. Chicagoans supported an art museum called the Chicago Academy of Fine Arts by 1879. In 1882, the name was changed to Art Institute of Chicago, and in 1893, the collection was moved into its current home on North Michigan Avenue. Today, the much-expanded museum is home to one of the world's leading collections of fine art.

The Field Museum of Natural History, John G. Shedd Aquarium, Museum of Science and Industry, and Adler Planetarium were all

MUSIC AND ART

made possible primarily through large donations, many by executives of onetime local retailing behemoths Sears, Roebuck & Co. and Marshall Field's. Donations keep most museums afloat, but an entity called Museums in the Park, through an annual tax approved back in 1903, helps support the care and maintenance of ten museums in Chicago's parks: Art Institute, Field Museum, Adler Planetarium, Shedd Aquarium, Chicago History Museum, Chicago Academy of Sciences, Museum of Science and Industry, DuSable Museum of African American History, Mexican Fine Arts Center Museum, and National Museum of Puerto Rican Arts and Culture.

Fact BOX

The word "mural" comes from the Latin for wall. Chicago's murals, large-scale painted or mosaic artwork, can be found on walls around the city. Two neighborhoods shine with murals: Mexican-influenced murals in Pilsen, on the Near South Side, and Puerto Rican-inspired artwork on the Near North Side, along Division Street near Humboldt Park.

"City of big shoulders, city on the make"

Carl Sandburg, Nelson Algren describe Chicago to the world

One of Chicago's most important literary journalists, Carl Sandburg, described in poetry the city of the early twentieth century. Following youthful meanderings throughout the country, when he lived as a hobo and took jobs as a janitor, a police reporter, a fireman, and a magazine writer, he landed in Chicago, where he solidified his socialist ideals.

Sandburg emerged as a poet and published *Chicago Poems* in 1916. One of its works, "Chicago," labeled the city "Hog Butcher for the World" and "City of Big Shoulders," names that stuck. He wrote poetry about tired shopgirls, sweatshops, and painted women, poetry that reflected the city but shocked genteel readers. Reporting

 JOURNALISM AND LITERATURE

for the *Chicago Daily News,* Sandburg covered the race riots in the city in 1919 and effectively described Chicago's segregated living in his contemporary account, *The Chicago Race Riots.*

In the mid-twentieth century, Nelson Algren was among the writers who brought realism to Chicago literature, describing the consequences of industrialism and the rise of big business on the lives of working-class people. In a 2016 Algren biography, *A Life, Chicago Tribune* writer Mary Wisniewski describes Algren as a "tireless champion of the downtrodden" who spent much of his life "palling around with the sorts of drug addicts, prostitutes, and poor laborers who inspired and populated his novels and short stories."

Algren is known for his novel *The Man with the Golden Arm,* which won the first National Book Award, in 1950. Wisniewski reveals more, explaining how Algren presented Chicago, "the city on the make," to the rest of the world.

Fact BOX

Chicago's newest museum is the American Writers Museum on North Michigan Avenue near the Chicago River, which features authors from across the United States. But one room is set aside for an exhibit on Chicago's writers, including both Sandburg and Algren.

Minority authors reflect the city

Richard Wright, Gwendolyn Brooks, and Sandra Cisneros

Chicago's literary history includes many minority artists, authors, painters, and poets. They reveal Chicago's minority experience to America, depicting the city's life and work, its residents' struggles and successes.

From the Depression arose a black literary output rivaled only by that of the Harlem Renaissance. Between 1925 and 1950, Chicago Black Renaissance writers, such as Richard Wright, focused on "literary naturalism," realistic portrayals of Chicago ghetto life. For instance, Wright's *Native Son* tells of Bigger Thomas, whose dreams of success are thwarted by society.

Gwendolyn Brooks, one of the city's most important poets, gave a voice to the city's African American residents. Works such as "Beverly Hills, Chicago," "The Children of the Poor," and the *Annie*

 JOURNALISM AND LITERATURE

Allen collection, earned Brooks the 1950 Pulitzer Prize. Her 1945 *In a Street in Bronzeville* portrayed everyday living in Chicago's African American ghetto, while *In the Mecca* spoke more specifically of a huge apartment complex, now demolished.

Sandra Cisneros is one of many authors and poets who portray the dilemmas of immigrants alienated from the city by language as well as tradition, notes author Bill Savage. Born in Chicago, Cisneros was brought up in the city but spent considerable time in her ancestral home in Mexico. Her 1984 *The House on Mango Street* tells the story of a young Latina coming of age in Chicago. Her numerous depictions of immigrants in an alien culture are collected in *Women Hollering Creek and Other Stories* (1991) and in her poetry collections. Cisneros was awarded a National Medal of Arts in 2015.

A comma before and, and other rules

Chicago in the nineteenth century was the US printing center. Along with presses that turned out mail-order catalogs were publishers of telephone books, pamphlets, and mailers.

The era ended when information began to be found more easily in digital form than on paper. Yet, university presses continued strong. Northwestern, DePaul, and Loyola universities as well as the University of Illinois and University of Chicago all have in-house publishing arms. While each has its special niche, it is at the University of Chicago where the famous *Chicago Manual of Style* was born.

The U of C Press opened its doors in 1891, employing typesetters who composed the print from hand-written manuscripts

 JOURNALISM AND LITERATURE

176

and proofreaders who came in to correct typos and edit for inconsistencies. That led to the compilation of a common set of editorial rules, or style sheet. By 1903, the style sheet was important enough to be included among items in the cornerstone of the new Press Building on the campus.

The sheet grew into a pamphlet, and, by 1906, a book. Its full title was *Manual of Style: Being a compilation of the typographical rules in force at the University of Chicago Press, to which are appended specimens of type in use.* Today, in its 17th edition, which includes instructions for the role of computers and digital references, *The Chicago Manual of Style* has become the authoritative reference work for authors, editors, copywriters, graphic designers, and publishers, and the work is known worldwide. It is available in both print and digital versions.

Hot off the presses

Chicago's newspaper legacy

Chicago's newspapers have been "in the news" since the first, the *Chicago Weekly Democrat*, appeared in 1833, four years before Chicago incorporated as a city. Through the years, more than two dozen English language daily newspapers were published in the city, with another twenty daily foreign language sheets. Today, awash in radio, TV, web news, and nonstop social media posts, Chicago is served by only two daily newspapers plus a variety of weekly and monthly publications aimed at specific populations.

According to the late journalism professor and author Richard A. Schwarzlose, Chicago had a newspaper climate consistently nurtured by four traditions: combative partisanship, competitive journalism, handsome design, and noteworthy reporters and writers, particularly columnists.

 JOURNALISM AND LITERATURE

OUR LIBERTY DEPENDS ON THE FREEDOM OF THE PRESS AND THAT CAN NOT BE LIMITED WITHOUT BEING LOST. THOMAS JEFFERSON

TO THE PRESS ALONE CHECKERED AS IT IS WITH ABUSES THE WORLD IS INDEBTED

The *Chicago Tribune* has influenced Chicago and national politics since its 1840s inception. Emphatic editors and publishers provided strong support for the Republican Party beginning with the Civil War; for the establishment of a convention center (later named after *Tribune* publisher Robert McCormick) on Lake Michigan; and against city or state governing bodies, particularly those of Democratic administrations, when the paper's investigations found fraud, clout, or patronage.

The *Chicago Sun-Times*, founded in the 1920s as the *Chicago Sun* but with a predecessor paper that dated to the 1840s, was long a liberal counterpoint to the *Tribune*. In 2017, beset by serious financial challenges, the paper was purchased by a consortium of liberal Chicagoans and labor unions promising a return to editorial support for the working classes.

From *Front Page* to Mike Royko

The Front Page, a comedy set in the 1920s and written by Ben Hecht and Charles MacArthur, two former Chicago newspaper reporters, featured working newsmen. "These reporters are biased, bigoted, racist, hate women, and are ruthless in their pursuit of the headline—and therefore are entirely recognizable characters," wrote one critic. The play, a hit on Broadway and later in the movies, presented Chicago's newsmen as tarnished heroes, uncovering the dirt of the day.

In real life, columnist Mike Royko, winner of the 1972 Pulitzer Prize for commentary, wrote 7,500 daily columns for three newspapers during his thirty-year career. First at the *Chicago Daily News*, then the *Chicago Sun-Times*, and finally the *Chicago Tribune*, Royko was a humorist, a critic, and author of *Boss*, a 1971 critical

 JOURNALISM AND LITERATURE

biography of Chicago Mayor Richard J. Daley. Royko acted as the city's conscience.

Like some other columnists, Royko created fictitious people with whom to carry on conversations, the most famous being Slats Grobnik, a stereotypical working-class Polish Chicagoan. Slats could not fathom Chicago politics, using immigrant logic to poke holes in political rhetoric.

Other columnists focused on sports and society gossip. Irv Kupcinet, known as "Kup," wrote a *Sun-Times* column that introduced boldface names, highlighting society and entertainment celebrities. He also hosted a late-night TV show, bringing the same people he wrote about into a studio for conversation. At one time, too, Kup was the color commentator for football's Chicago Bears, involving himself in two of Chicagoans' favorite pastimes, sports and entertainment.

City of steeples

Chicago's religious institutions

Chicago's settlers and immigrants brought their religious beliefs with them, and their many houses of worship helped shape the city.

Churches and synagogues anchored the middle-class communities that grew around downtown Chicago after the Civil War. Religious institutions were community anchors in most neighborhoods, providing spiritual uplift, certainly, but also helping residents find jobs, food, or housing, according to Christopher D. Cantwell, an author and University of Missouri–Kansas City professor of public history.

The Roman Catholic Church, in particular, aided the rapid spread of churches, as it assigned Irish, German, and Italian immigrants to different parishes, each with priests who spoke the

SACRED PLACES

immigrant language. The archdiocese's "national churches" policy was kept in place until the 1920s.

At the turn of the last century, many of the city's more than forty Orthodox Jewish synagogues were concentrated on the Near West Side, while the Catholic Archdiocese's seventy national parishes were in South and West Side neighborhoods, where laborers lived. Non-Catholic churches for Norwegians, Swedes, and Germans were found on the North Side.

African Americans who came up from the South during the Great Migration between the two world wars remade Chicago's religious landscape. Though some of their churches met in storefronts, many of the new congregations took over church and synagogue buildings left behind by ethnic groups that were moving farther west or south.

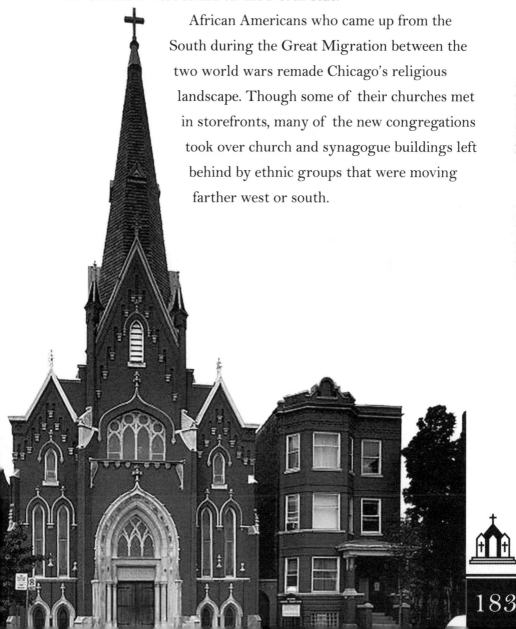

Churches and their architecture

Chicago's famed religious structures

Chicago's inventory of religious institutions is large. Among them are houses of worship with unusual architecture.

The Chicago Temple, or the First United Methodist Church of Chicago, stands across the street from Daley Plaza downtown. At 568 feet, it is the world's tallest church building. The 1924 building designed by Chicago architecture firm Holabird & Roche is a neo-Gothic monument to Methodism and the parish's commitment to the city. The tower encompasses the Sky Chapel and an outdoor patio at the highest levels, a ground-floor sanctuary, and office space in between. Office rents support church operations.

Surrounded by seven acres of gardens, the Baha'i House of Worship in north suburban Wilmette is one of eight temples of the Baha'i faith worldwide, the only one in North America.

SACRED PLACES

Completed in 1953, it is the oldest surviving Baha'i House of
Worship in the world. From a height of 191 feet, the domed,
lacy white structure designed by architects Louis Bourgeois and
George A. Fuller stands out for miles.

In the Ukrainian Village neighborhood on the Near West
Side, architect Louis Sullivan's Holy Trinity Cathedral, the
Midwest cathedral of the Orthodox Church, is both a spiritual
and architectural icon. Impressed by a model at the 1893 World's
Columbian Exposition, Father John Kochurov, a young priest
from St. Petersburg who was starting a new church to serve the
growing Chicago population of Russians, Serbs, and Greeks, hired
Sullivan. The famed architect's inspiration was a small wooden
church in Tatarskaya, Siberia. The cathedral's cornerstone was
laid on March 31, 1902.

How green is my prairie?

From its inception, Chicago has honored green space almost to the point of worship.

In the city's 1837 incorporation, the downtown lakefront was considered "open and free." Later, in the Progressive era of the late nineteenth century, a "green necklace," or string of parks on the city's perimeter, was created for several reasons: to provide open space for tenement residents who had few outdoor places to go in their crowded neighborhoods, to provide fieldhouses with bathing facilities for residents who lacked indoor plumbing, and to create aesthetically pleasing spaces in the city.

Forest Preserve District of Cook County

www.fpdcc.com

Across the city, individual park commissions accumulated land, resulting in the South Side's Jackson and Washington parks; the West Side's Humboldt, Douglas, and Garfield parks; and the

SACRED PLACES

North Side's Lincoln Park. City parks were later consolidated under the Chicago Park District, which still controls them. Today, parks usually include playgrounds and playfields and offer programs that include summer camps, after-school sports, and nature study.

In line with concepts in architect Daniel Burnham's *1909 Plan of Chicago*, the development of the park system was followed by the creation of forest preserves on the outskirts of the city in areas of Cook County. Today, the County Forest Preserve Board (composed of members of the Cook County Board) manages the forest preserves, which offer nature centers; water activities, such as canoeing and kayaking on branches of the Chicago River; and camping.

Fact BOX

The 606, a twenty-first century linear park, is a $95 million elevated bike and walking trail created from abandoned railroad land on the city's Northwest Side. The 2.7-mile Bloomingdale Trail is included, as is a series of street-level parks. Opened in 2015 and a quick success, The 606 is already slated for expansion.

From Victorian picnics to soldier memorials

Chicago's three largest cemeteries predate the Civil War. Popular during Victorian times as a Sunday picnic destination, today they serve as museums, telling Chicago's story through gravestones, mausoleums, and memorials.

Graceland, opened in 1860, is the final resting place of some of Chicago's most prominent residents. The 119-acre cemetery was designed in a naturalistic style by Ossian Simonds. Tombs of businessman Potter Palmer and department store magnate Marshall Field are here, along with the grave of architect-planner Daniel

SACRED PLACES

Burnham. Also highlighted are architect-designed mausoleums, including Louis Sullivan's Getty Tomb, built for the wife of a Chicago lumber baron.

Graceland is the final resting place of Chicagoans reburied from the city's first cemetery, in Lincoln Park, as is Rosehill Cemetery, on the city's North Side. Among Rosehill's memorials are those of 230 Union soldiers and nearly fifty officers from the Civil War, as well as founders of the Republican Party. The 350-acre cemetery dates to 1859. Its landscape was designed by William Saunders. William Boyington, one of Chicago's first architects, designed the imposing main gate.

Oak Woods Cemetery, on the South Side, also has ties to the Civil War. The Confederate Mound is the final resting place of more than four thousand Confederate soldiers—captured in battle and sent to Camp Douglas, a nearby Union prisoner-of-war camp, where they died of injury, illness, or malnutrition. Oak Woods also tells a second story: Among those buried there are Chicago's first African American mayor, Harold Washington, and many African American leaders who were in the forefront of last century's civil rights movement.

BIBLIOGRAPHY

Books

Borzo, Greg. *The Chicago "L".* Charleston, S.C.: Arcadia Publishing, 2007.

City of Chicago Department of Development and Planning, Lewis W. Hill, Commissioner. *Historic City: The Settlement of Chicago.* Chicago: City of Chicago, n/d.

Chicago Tribune Staff, Stevenson Swanson, ed. *Chicago Days: 150 Moments in the Life of a Great City.* Wheaton, Illinois: Cantigny First Division Foundation, 1997.

Cromie, Robert. *A Short History of Chicago.* San Francisco: Lexikos, 1984.

Duis, Perry. *Chicago: Creating New Traditions.* Chicago: Chicago Historical Society, 1976.

Geary, Rick. *The Beast of Chicago: The Murderous Career of H.H. Holmes.* New York: Nantier, Beall, Minoustchine Publishing Inc., 2003

Gray, Mary Lackritz. *A Guide to Chicago's Murals.* Chicago and London: University of Chicago Press: 2001.

Grossman, James R., Ann Durkin Keating, and Janice L. Reiff, eds. *The Encyclopedia of Chicago.* Chicago and London: The University of Chicago Press: 2004 The Newberry Library.

Hayner, Don and Tom McNamee. *Streetwise Chicago: A History of Chicago Street Names.* Chicago: Loyola University Press, 1988.

Heise, Kennan and Mark Frazel. *Hands on Chicago: Getting Hold of the City (Special Chicago 150th Birthday Edition).* Chicago: Bonus Books, 1987.

Johnson, Lorraine and John Ryan, main contributors. *Eyewitness Travel Guide: Chicago.* London: DK Dorling Kindersley Ltd., A Penguin Co. 2006.

Larson, Mark Henry and Bob Boone. *Write Through Chicago.* Chicago: Amika Press, 2013.

McBrien, Judith Paine. *Pocket Guide to Chicago Architecture.* New York: W.W. Norton & Co., 1997.

McClelland, Edward. *How To Speak Midwestern.* Cleveland, Ohio: Belt Publishing, 2016.

Miller, Donald L. *City of the Century: The Epic of Chicago and the Making of America.* New York: Touchstone, 1966.

N/A, *Michelin Green Guide: Chicago.* Greenville, S.C.: Michelin Travel Publications, Michelin North America, 1996.

Page, Molly. *100 Things to Do in Chicago Before You Die.* St. Louis: Reedy Press, LLC., 2016.

Parnell, Sean. *Historic Bars of Chicago.* Chicago: Lake Claremont Press, 2010.

Poppeliers, John C. and S. Allen Chambers Jr., Historic American Buildings Survey. *What Style Is It: A guide to American Architecture.* Hoboken, N. J.: John Wiley & Sons, 2003.

Price, Virginia B., David A. Spatz, and D. Bradford Hunt, eds. *Out of the Loop Chicago: Vernacular Architecture Forum.* Chicago: Vernacular Architecture Forum, 2015.

Pridmore, Jay. *Marshall Field's A building book from the Chicago Architecture Foundation.* Petaluma, CAF: Pomegranate Communications, Inc., 2002.

Robinson, Guy. *Do You Know? (sic) Chicago* Naperville, Ill.: Sourcebooks, Inc., © 2008 by Carlinsky and Carlinsky, Inc.

Selzer, Adam. *Chronicles of Old Chicago: Exploring the History and Lore of the Windy City.* (New York: Museyon, Inc., 2014)

Sinkevitch, Alice and Laurie McGovern Petersen, editors. *AIA Guide to Chicago Third Edition.* Urbana, Chicago, and Springfield: University of Illinois Press, 2014.

Solomonson, Katherine. *The Chicago Tribune Tower Competition: Skyscraper Design and Cultural Change in the 1920s.* Chicago: The University of Chicago Press, 2001.

Solzman, David M. *The Chicago River: An Illustrated History and Guide to the River and Its Waterways.* Chicago: Wild Onion Books, an imprint of Loyola Press, 1998.

Taylor, Troy. *Weird Illinois.* New York: Sterling Publishing Co., Inc.; Barnes and Noble Publishing, Inc. 2005.

Thompson, Lowell. *African Americans in Chicago*, Charleston, South Carolina: Arcadia Publishing, 2012.

Tiebert, Laura. *Frommer's Chicago Day by Day (1ˢᵗ Edition)*. Hoboken, N. J.: Wiley Publishing Inc., 2006.

Newspapers, magazines, and other periodicals

Chiarella, Tom. "The World's Best Urban Gondola Ride: What I learned from traveling every inch of the L in one day." *Chicago magazine*, March 2017.

Chu, Louisa. "Iconic South Side cake will blow your mind." *Chicago Tribune*, March 15, 2017.

Frost, Peter. "Like craft beer? You're in the right city." *Crain's Chicago Business*, March 17, 2017.

Glanton, Dahleen. "Chance reminds us: Black boys are worth fighting for." *Chicago Tribune*, July 3, 2017.

Kamin, Blair. "Public art's startling vulnerability on display." *Chicago Tribune*, April 2, 2017.

Lee, William. "Hundreds attend Muddy Waters mural dedication." *Chicago Tribune*, June 9, 2017.

Loerzel, Robert. "In a divided Chicago, one thing we all agree on: A damn fine flag." *Crain's Chicago Business*, April 4, 2017.

Loerzel, Robert. "Chicago's Flag Is a Much Bigger Deal Than Any Other City's Flag." *Chicago Tribune*, Aug. 22, 2013.

Smith, Ryan. "RIP Wrigleyville. Welcome to Rickettsville. *Chicago Reader*, April 6, 2017.

Young, Kristin and Genesis Villarreal. "Navy Pier: Fast Facts," *Navy Pier: the second century begins*, Navy Pier, Inc., Summer 2017.

Websites

Crapanzano, Christina. "The Second City" Dec. 16, 2009. http://content.time.com/time/arts/article/0,8599,1948114,00.html.

Dixler, Hillary. "The Italian Beef Sandwich at Al's in Chicago," EATER, July 8, 2014. http://www.eater.com2014/7/8/6198993/the-italian-beef-sandwich.

Gerzina, Daniel, "An Eater's Guide to Chicago: Unofficial, highly opinionated information about the Windy City," May 26, 2017. https://chicagoeater.com2016/9/19/1253944/Chicago-city-guide-where-to-eat-drink

Peterson, Dan. Life's Little Mysteries Contributor. "How the NFL Football Got Its Shape." Sept. 8, 2010. https://www.livescience.com/32808-nfl-football-spheroid-origins.html

http://mentalfloss.com/article/55060/how-chicagos-neighborhoods-got-their-names

http://oldtownchicago.org/history-archive/the-second-city-a-brief-history

http://openhousechicago.org/sites/site/chicago-temple-first-united-methodist-church

http://www.garrettpopcorn.com/garrett-popcorn-shops/our-story

http://www.thechicago77.com/chicago-neighborhoods/

https://holytrinitycathedral.net/history.html

https://www.britannica.com/biography/Sandra-Cisneros

http://www.chicagoreviewpress.com/algren-products-9781613735329.php

http://www.chicagomanualofstyle.org/about16_history.html

http://www.chicagomag.com/city-life/November-2014/Chicago-neighborhoods

http://www.choosechicago.com/blog/post/the-history-of-gospel-music-in-chicago

http://www.viennabeef.com/history-hot-dog-culture

http://www.wbez.org/Curious City, May 2017

PHOTO CREDITS

INDEX